Wisdom, Merit, and Purification Through the Blessing of the 35 Buddhas

A Text for Daily Practice

Compiled by the 14th Shamar Rinpoche

with translation by Pamela Gayle White

Second edition (hardcover)
Bird of Paradise Press
Lexington, Virginia

Wisdom, Merit, and Purification Through the Blessing of the 35 Buddhas: A Text for Daily Practice

ISBN: 978-1-7347823-5-6
Library of Congress Control Number: 2021933476

General Editor: Gregory Mock
Cover painting by Huai Shion Chen
Booklet design & illustrations by Judah Lynn
Modified & adapted for second edition hardcover format by Bird of Paradise Press

Bird of Paradise Press
1223 N. Lee Highway, #250
Lexington, Virginia, 24450 USA
birdofparadisepress.org

Compiled by the 14th Shamar Rinpoche
with translation by Pamela Gayle White

Contents

Dedication

This practice text is dedicated to peace in the world.
It is also dedicated to the prosperity of the Buddhist Kingdom of Bhutan— the country that has given me the opportunity to generate teachings in this world.

— Shamar Rinpoche

Introduction by the 14th Shamar Rinpoche

Buddha Shakyamuni gave the 35 Buddhas Sutra as the most effective and expedient method for purifying negativities and accumulating merit. The practice was very widespread in Buddhist India, especially during the time when the Mahayana and Vajrayana—the paths of the Bodhisattva—were flourishing there. Many Buddhists—yogis of the tantric lineages, scholars in Nalanda University, monks and nuns, householder practitioners—chose this sutra among all of the available Mahayana sutras and tantras as their preliminary practice or daily practice. Indeed, the great Tibetan master Marpa Lhodrakpa and a number of his peers chose it as their preliminary practice before focusing on the advanced practices of the Vajrayana.

The 35 Buddhas Sutra, also called the Daily Confession in Three Sets, or Arya Triskandhaka Sutra, is particularly timely for today's practitioners. The Buddha himself taught it in Shravasti; it belongs to his second cycle of teachings. A pure, authentic and non-sectarian transmission, it is unsullied by controversy or partisanship on any level. A vehicle of great blessing, it is appropriate for beginning and advanced practitioners alike.

The text presented in this book provides a comprehensive practice text based on the 35 Buddhas Sutra. In addition to the sutra text itself, the book also includes the mandala offering (present in many Mahayana sutras and tantras), as well as other selected prayers from different sources. For example, the Bodhisattva vow is from Shantideva, the invitation and dedication are from the sutras, and the last four verses of the text are a traditional prayer recited by lamas throughout Tibet. The intent of this book is to provide a complete text suitable for daily practice by a wide variety of students of all lineages.

Those who wish to practice this sutra should receive explanations from an authentic teacher of their lineage. While it is possible to begin the practice and familiarize oneself with it without having received them, one cannot truly approach the heart of the practice nor receive its full blessing until the explanations and reading transmission have been requested and obtained. As a sutra practice, it does not focus on a tutelary deity (***yidam***) from the tantras, and therefore there is no corresponding empowerment (***wang***).

The 35 Buddhas Sutra Practice can be practiced individually or with a group. It can be recited occasionally, daily, or as a preliminary practice (***ngöndro***). Here, confession and prostrations are done before the 35 Buddhas, and the mandala offering is also incorporated into the practice. In the context of the preliminary practices, prostrations and the mandala offering would be followed by the Vajrasattva purification practice and finally the Guru Yoga with Avalokiteshvara, or Chenrezi—the great Bodhisattva of compassion—as the basis for developing devotion and reinforcing our connection with enlightenment.

In former times, many great practitioners, retreatants, and lay people have benefited greatly from the 35 Buddhas Sutra. Today also, many benefits will be obtained by relying on this practice of the great masters of the past. The efforts of sincere practitioners will be rewarded by success in their chosen practice. Practitioners will be protected from life-threatening obstacles and from karmic mistakes and hindrances. The negative karma of body, speech, and mind will be purified. Well-being and happiness will be experienced spontaneously.

For all of these reasons, I have chosen to revive this precious practice and make it a standard in Bodhi Path centers throughout the world. The Bodhi Path curriculum offers a variety of main paths of practice to suit the needs and inspiration of different practitioners. The 35 Buddhas Sutra Practice is an appropriate starting point for all of these paths. After completion of at least 10,000 prostrations to the Buddhas and 10,000 mandala offerings, students may receive teachings on many of the other practices belonging to the Bodhi Path curriculum, or they may choose to continue to focus on this as their main practice.

The 35 Buddhas prostrations and mandala offerings may also be undertaken as preliminary practices (***ngöndro***) that precede more advanced Vajrayana practices, although there are other options for preliminary practice too. For example, practitioners who follow the Kagyu Mahamudra path can choose to begin with this 35 Buddhas Sutra Practice or the Tsoknyi Zungjuk, the Union of the Two Accumulations practice previously compiled by me and based on the instructions of Mikyö Dorjé, the 8th Karmapa, as contained in his book Dhag gyu Dragyen. Those who are committed to the Karma Kagyu Mahamudra Path can choose between the 35 Buddhas practice and the Mahamudra Preliminaries as taught by Wangchuk Dorje, the 9th Karmapa. In any case, as a preliminary practice, students must complete 100,000 prostrations and 100,000 mandala offerings, as well as 100,000 Vajrasattva purification mantras and guru yoga recitations.

When we confess all of our negativities in front of the 35 Buddhas, confidence in the power of the practice is of paramount importance. Just as all negative actions leave an imprint in the mindstream that blocks positive karma from ripening and reinforces the illusion of samsara, the merit generated by this practice blocks negative karma from ripening and sets us firmly on the path to liberation.

Chokyi Lodro, 14th Shamarpa

Preliminary Prayers

Praise of the Buddha and his Twelve Deeds

Refuge

The Four Immeasurables

Blessing the Place

Request to Come and Stay

The Seven Branch Prayer

ཐུབ་པའི་མཛད་པ་བཅུ་གཉིས་ལ་བཞུགས་སོ།
Praise of the Buddha and his Twelve Deeds

This prayer reminds us of the qualities of Buddha Shakyamuni, the Buddha of our era, who is the source of the practice that follows. Being aware of his deeds and qualities allows great blessing to ripen in our mindstream. This prayer is not inluded in the original text and, unlike the other sections, it needn't be recited each time we do the practice.

1) ཐབས་མཁས་ཐུགས་རྗེས་ཤཱཀྱའི་རིགས་སུ་འཁྲུངས། གཞན་གྱིས་མི་ཐུབ་
Tab khé tuk jé shakyé rik su trung / Shen gyi mi tub
བདུད་ཀྱི་དཔུང་འཇོམས་པ། གསེར་གྱི་ལྷུན་པོ་ལྟ་བུར་བརྗིད་པའི་སྐུ།
dükyi pung jom pa / Ser gyi lhünpo tabur jipé ku /
ཤཱཀྱའི་རྒྱལ་པོ་ཁྱོད་ལ་ཕྱག་འཚལ་ལོ།
Shakyé gyalpo kyöla chak tsallo //

1) King of the Shakyas, I bow down before you
whose appearance is as glorious as a mountain of gold.
Expressing your skillful methods and wisdom,
you took birth within the lineage of the Shakyas;
you conquered Mara's armies where others could not.

2) གང་གིས་དང་པོར་བྱང་ཆུབ་ཐུགས་བསྐྱེད་ནས། བསོད་ནམས་ཡེ་ཤེས་
Gang gi tangpor jangchub tuk kyé né / Sönam yéshé
ཚོགས་གཉིས་རྫོགས་མཛད་ཅིང་། དུས་འདིར་མཛད་པ་རྒྱ་ཆེན་འགྲོ་བ་ཡི།
tsok nyi dzok dzé ching / Dü dir dzépa gya chen drowa yi /
མགོན་གྱུར་ཁྱོད་ལ་བདག་གིས་བསྟོད་པར་བགྱི།
Gön gyur kyöla dagi tö par gyi //

2) By first developing awakened mind in all situations,
you completed the accumulations of merit and wisdom.
Now, through your all-embracing enlightened activity,
you are the guardian of beings: Protector, I praise you.

3) ལྷ་རྣམས་དོན་མཛད་འདུལ་བའི་དུས་མཁྱེན་ནས། ལྷ་ལས་བབས་ནས་
Lhanam döndzé dülwé dü kyen né / Lhalé babné
གླང་ཆེན་ལྟར་གཤེགས་ཤིང་། རིགས་ལ་གཟིགས་ནས་ལྷ་མོ་སྒྱུ་འཕྲུལ་གྱི།
langchen tar shék shing/ Rikla zikné lhamo gyu trül gyi /
ལྷུམས་སུ་ཞུགས་པར་མཛད་ལ་ཕྱག་འཚལ་ལོ།
Lhum su shukpar dzéla chak tsallo //

3) I bow down before you, who while helping the devas,
saw that the time to tame us was finally at hand.
Coming from the god realms, you appeared as an elephant;
Knowing her nobility, you entered Maya-Devi's womb.

4) ཟླ་བ་བཅུ་རྫོགས་ཤཱཀྱའི་སྲས་པོ་ནི། བཀྲ་ཤིས་ལུམྦིའི་ཚལ་དུ་
Dawa chu dzok shakyé sépo ni/ Tashi lumbi'i tsaldu
བལྟམས་པའི་ཚེ། ཚངས་དང་བརྒྱ་བྱིན་གྱིས་བསྟོད་མཚན་མཆོག་ནི།
tampé tsé / Tsang tang gyajin gyi tö tsen chok ni /
བྱང་ཆུབ་རིགས་སུ་ངེས་མཛད་ཕྱག་འཚལ་ལོ།
Jangchub riksu ngédzé chak tsallo//

4) I bow down before you, the prince of the Shakyas,
born ten months later in Lumbini's happy grove.

At that time, Indra and Brahma both praised you,
and your exceptional marks confirmed with certainty
that you belonged to the lineage of the enlightened ones.

5) གཞོན་ནུ་སྟོབས་ལྡན་མི་ཡི་སེང་གེ་དེས། ཨཾ་ག་མ་ག་དྷར་ནི་
Shönnu tobden miyi sengé dé / Anga maga dharni
སྒྱུ་རྩལ་བསྟན། སྐྱེ་བོ་དྲེགས་པ་ཅན་རྣམས་ཚར་བཅད་ནས།
gyu tsal ten / Kyéwo drékpa chennam tsar ché né /
འགྲན་ཟླ་མེད་པར་མཛད་ལ་ཕྱག་འཚལ་ལོ།
Drenda mépar dzé la chak tsallo //

5) I bow down before you, invincible, unrivaled;
the powerful youth, the lion among men.
By proving your skills in Anga and Magadha,
you fully defeated your haughty opponents.

6) འཇིག་རྟེན་ཆོས་དང་མཐུན་པར་བྱ་བ་དང་། ཁ་ན་མ་ཐོ་
Jikten chötang tünpar jawa tang / Khana mato
སྤང་ཕྱིར་བཙུན་མོ་ཡི། འཁོར་དང་ལྡན་མཛད་ཐབས་ལ་མཁས་པ་ཡིས།
pangchir tsünmo yi / Khortang dendzé tabla khépa yi
རྒྱལ་སྲིད་སྐྱོང་བར་མཛད་ལ་ཕྱག་འཚལ་ལོ།
Gyalsi kyongwar dzéla chak tsallo //

6) I bow down before you, who with skillful means
acted in accordance with the ways of the world:
you wed an irreproachable queen, with her retinue,
and wielded the scepter within your kingdom.

7) འཁོར་བའི་བྱ་བ་སྙིང་པོ་མེད་གཟིགས་ནས། ཁྱིམ་ནས་བྱུང་སྟེ་མཁའ་ལ་
Khorwé jawa nyingpo mé zik né / Kyim né jung té khala
གཤེགས་ནས་ཀྱང་། མཆོད་རྟེན་རྣམ་དག་དྲུང་དུ་ཉིད་ལ་ཉིད།
shék né kyang / Chöten namdak drungdu nyi la nyi/
རབ་ཏུ་བྱུང་བར་མཛད་ལ་ཕྱག་འཚལ་ལོ།
Rabtu jungwar dzé la chak tsallo //

7) I bow down before you, the perfect renunciant;
you saw clearly the vanity of worldly pursuits.
Having left your home you arose into the sky,
then settled just in front of the Namdak Stupa.

8) བརྩོན་པས་བྱང་ཆུབ་བསྒྲུབ་པར་དགོངས་ནས་ནི། ནེ་རཉྫ་ནའི་
Tsönpé jangchub drupar gong né ni / Néran dzané
འགྲམ་དུ་ལོ་དྲུག་ཏུ། དཀའ་བ་སྤྱད་མཛད་བརྩོན་འགྲུས་མཐར་ཕྱིན་པས།
dramdu lo druk tu / Kawa ché dzé tsöndrü tarchin pé /
བསམ་གཏན་མཆོག་བརྙེས་མཛད་ལ་ཕྱག་འཚལ་ལོ།
Samten chok nyé dzéla chak tsallo//

8) I bow down before you who became an ascetic
intent on attaining liberation through hardship.
During six years on the banks of the river Nairanjana,
your only practice was the perfection of perseverance
until you reached samadhi: supreme meditative stability.

9) ཐོག་མ་མེད་ནས་འབད་པ་དོན་ཡོད་ཕྱིར། མ་ག་དྷཱ་ཡི་བྱང་ཆུབ་
Tokma méné bépa dön yö chir / Magadhayi jangchub
ཤིང་དྲུང་དུ། སྐྱིལ་ཀྲུང་མི་གཡོ་མངོན་པར་སངས་རྒྱས་ནས།
shing drung du / Kyiltrung miyo ngönpar sangyé né /
བྱང་ཆུབ་རྫོགས་པར་མཛད་ལ་ཕྱག་འཚལ་ལོ།
Jangchub dzokpar dzéla chak tsallo //

9) I bow down before you who always endeavored
to achieve the sole purpose that would have true meaning.
Beneath the Bodhi tree in the realm of Magadha
you sat with your legs crossed, steadfast and firm,
and became the Buddha, the Fully Awakened One.

10) ཐུགས་རྗེས་འགྲོ་ལ་མྱུར་དུ་གཟིགས་ནས་ནི། ཝཱ་རཱ་ཎ་སཱི་ལ་སོགས་
Tuk jé drola nyurdu zikné ni / Varanasi laso
གནས་མཆོག་ཏུ། ཆོས་ཀྱི་འཁོར་ལོ་བསྐོར་ནས་གདུལ་བྱ་རྣམས།
néchok tu / Chökyi khorlo korné dül ja nam /
ཐེག་པ་གསུམ་ལ་འགོད་མཛད་ཕྱག་འཚལ་ལོ།
Tékpa sumla gödzé chak tsallo //

10) I bow down before you, who at once beheld beings
with such great compassion that in many sacred places,
such as Varanasi, you turned the wheel of the Dharma
and set your disciples on the paths of the three yanas.

11) གཞན་གྱི་རྒོལ་བ་ངན་པ་ཚར་གཅོད་ཕྱིར། མུ་སྟེགས་སྟོན་པ་
Shen gyi gölwa ngenpa tsar chö chir / Muték tönpa
དྲུག་དང་ལྷ་སྦྱིན་སོགས། འཁོར་མོ་འཇིག་གི་ཡུལ་དུ་བདུད་རྣམས་བཏུལ།
druk tang lhajin so / Khormo jik gi yüldu dünam tül /
ཐུབ་པ་གཡུལ་ལས་རྒྱལ་ལ་ཕྱག་འཚལ་ལོ།
Tubpa yüllé gyal la chak tsallo //

11) I bow down before you, victor of all battles,
sage who overcame the hostilities of challengers
–the six heretical teachers, Devadatta, and others–
through subjugating the Maras in the land of Varanasi.

12) སྲིད་པ་གསུམ་ན་དཔེ་མེད་ཡོན་ཏན་གྱིས། མཉན་དུ་ཡོད་པར་
Sipa sum na pémé yönten gyi / Nyendu yöpar
ཆོ་འཕྲུལ་ཆེན་པོ་བསྟན། ལྷ་མི་འགྲོ་བ་ཀུན་གྱིས་རབ་མཆོད་པ།
chotrül chenpo ten / Lhami drowa kungyi rab chö pa /
བསྟན་པ་རྒྱས་པར་མཛད་ལ་ཕྱག་འཚལ་ལོ།
Tenpa gyépar dzéla chak tsallo //

12) I bow down before you who spread the Holy Teachings,
inspiring the reverence of gods, humans, and all beings.
Using your skills, unequaled within the three spheres,
you taught in Shravasti with great magical displays.

13) ལེ་ལོ་ཅན་རྣམས་ཆོས་ལ་བསྐུལ་བྱའི་ཕྱིར། རྩ་མཆོག་གྲོང་གི་
Lélo chennam chöla kül jé chir / Tsa chok drong gi
ས་གཞི་གཙང་མ་རུ། འཆི་མེད་རྡོ་རྗེ་ལྟ་བུའི་སྐུ་གཤེགས་ནས།
sashi tsang ma ru / Chimé dorjé tabu'i kushék né /
མྱ་ངན་འདའ་བར་མཛད་ལ་ཕྱག་འཚལ་ལོ།
Nya ngen dawar dzéla chak tsallo //

13) I bow down before you, whose parinirvana
serves to compel the indolent to practice the Dharma.
At the pure place, the town of Kushinagara,
you gave up your immortal, vajra-like body,
and manifested there the state beyond suffering.

14) ཡང་དག་ཉིད་དུ་འཇིག་པ་མེད་གཟིགས་ཀྱང་། མ་འོངས་སེམས་ཅན་
Yangdak nyidu jikpa mé zik kyang / Ma'ong semchen
བསོད་ནམས་ཐོབ་བྱའི་ཕྱིར། དེ་ཉིད་དུ་ནི་རིང་བསྲེལ་མང་སྤྲུལ་ནས།
sönam tob jé chir / Dényi duni ringsel mang trül né /
སྐུ་གདུང་ཆ་བརྒྱད་མཛད་ལ་ཕྱག་འཚལ་ལོ།
Kudung chagyé dzéla chak tsallo //

14) I bow down before you who gave the eight-fold relic.
Though you knew that, ultimately, nothing can perish,
you manifested a great number of relics in this world
so that sentient beings might gather merit thereafter.

ཞེས་པ་མགོན་པོ་ཀླུ་སྒྲུབ་ཀྱིས་མཛད་པའོ།
Composed by Lord Nagarjuna.

སྐྱབས་འགྲོ་ནི།
Refuge

Here we renew our refuge vow, reaffirming our confidence in the Buddha as the perfect teacher and ultimate state of awakening, the Dharma as the perfect body of teachings, and the Sangha as the perfect community of beings to guide and accompany us along the path to enlightenment.

བྱང་ཆུབ་སྙིང་པོར་མཆིས་ཀྱི་བར། །སངས་རྒྱས་རྣམས་ལ་སྐྱབས་སུ་མཆི།
Jangchub nyingpor chikyi bar / Sangyé namla kyab su chi/

ཆོས་དང་བྱང་ཆུབ་སེམས་དཔའ་ཡི། །ཚོགས་ལའང་དེ་བཞིན་སྐྱབས་སུ་མཆི།
Chö tang jangchub sempa yi / Tsok la'ang déshin kyab su chi//

Until I reach the heart of enlightenment,
I take refuge in the Buddhas.
Likewise, I take refuge in the Dharma
and in the assembly of Bodhisattvas.

ཞེས་ལན་གསུམ།
Repeat 3 times

ཚད་མེད་བཞི་ནི།
The Four Immeasurables

With this classic prayer, we reiterate our motivation as that of the Great Vehicle. The merit that results from any practice performed with this sincere motivation is immeasurably vast.

སེམས་ཅན་ཐམས་ཅད་བདེ་བ་དང་བདེ་བའི་རྒྱུ་དང་ལྡན་པར་གྱུར་ཅིག
Semchen tamché déwa tang déwé gyu tang denpar gyur chik /

སྡུག་བསྔལ་དང་སྡུག་བསྔལ་གྱི་རྒྱུ་དང་བྲལ་བར་གྱུར་ཅིག
Du'ngal tang du'ngal gyi gyu tang dralwar gyur chik /

སྡུག་བསྔལ་མེད་པའི་བདེ་བ་དམ་པ་དང་མི་འབྲལ་བར་གྱུར་ཅིག
Du'ngal mépé déwa dampa tang mindral war gyur chik /

ཉེ་རིང་ཆགས་སྡང་གཉིས་དང་བྲལ་བའི་བཏང་སྙོམས་ཆེན་པོ་ལ་
Nyéring chakdang nyi tang dralwé tang nyom chenpo la

གནས་པར་གྱུར་ཅིག
népar gyur chik //

May all beings find happiness and the cause of happiness.
May they be free from suffering and the cause of suffering.
May they not be separated from the perfect happiness
that is free from suffering.
May they abide in great impartiality,
free from attachment and aversion to those near and far.

ས་གཞི་བྱིན་རླབས་བརྒྱས་པ་ནི།
Blessing the Place

Our environment, whatever it may be, is produced by mind and mind alone. The manifestation known as samsara, the impure world we call our own, has its roots in the confused mind that mistakenly clings to a "self." Because of this attachment, we habitually put a great deal of effort and energy into making a comfortable environment for this "self," thus reinforcing our delusion.

Visualizing a pure realm for the Buddhas is the antidote to this tendency. By evoking the most beautiful paradise imaginable for the enlightened ones, we train in leaving behind our habitual yearnings for personal comfort and create the causes for future rebirth in the pure realms.

ཐམས་ཅད་དུ་ཡང་ས་གཞི་དག གསེག་མ་ལ་སོགས་མེད་པ་དང་།
Tamché duyang sashi dak / Sékma laso mépar tang /

ལག་མཐིལ་ལྟར་མཉམ་བཻ་ཌཱུར་ཡའི། རང་བཞིན་འཇམ་པོར་གནས་གྱུར་ཅིག
Lak til tar nyam bendur'yé / Rangshin jampor né gyur chik //

May the entire surface of the earth
be free from impurities such as pebbles.
May it be smooth like the palm of the hand,
and as lovely as Vaidurya crystal.

སྤྱན་འདྲེན་བཞུགས་གསོལ་ནི། Request to Come and Stay

As with Blessing the Place, we are training in cutting through habitual tendencies. Normally we are most concerned with calling and inviting those to whom we are attached in a worldly sense. Here we replace our worldly attachment with devotion based on our awareness of the qualities and blessings of the Buddhas.

མ་ལུས་སེམས་ཅན་ཀུན་གྱི་མགོན་གྱུར་ཅིང་། བདུད་སྡེ་དཔུང་བཅས་མི་བཟད་

Malü semchen küngyi gön gyur ching / Düdé pung ché mizé

འཇོམས་མཛད་ལྷ། དངོས་རྣམས་མ་ལུས་ཇི་བཞིན་མཁྱེན་གྱུར་པའི།

jom dzé lha / Ngönam malu jishin khyen gyur pé /

བཅོམ་ལྡན་འཁོར་བཅས་གནས་འདིར་གཤེགས་སུ་གསོལ།

Chomden khorché nédir shék su söl //

Protectors of all beings without exception,
divine ones who humbled the mighty maras and their hordes,
you who know each and every thing just as it is:
please come here with your entourage, Victorious Ones.

བཅོམ་ལྡན་འདིར་ནི་བྱོན་པ་ལེགས། བདག་ཅག་བསོད་ནམས་སྐལ་པར་ལྡན།

Chomden dir ni jönpa lék / Dachak sönam kalpar den /

བདག་གི་མཆོད་ཡོན་བཞེས་སླད་དུ། འདི་ཉིད་དུ་ནི་བཞུགས་སུ་གསོལ།

Dagi chöyön shélé du / Dini duni shuk su söl /

How wonderful that you have come, O Victorious Ones!
How incredibly fortunate are we!
Kindly remain here among us in order to receive our offerings.

སྟོང་གསུམ་ཀུན་དང་མཉམ་པ་ཡི། པདྨ་འདབ་བརྒྱད་གེ་སར་བཅས།

Tongsum kun tang nyampa yi / Péma dab gyé gésar ché /

བདེ་ཞིང་ཡངས་པར་འབུལ་ལགས་ན། ཅི་བདེ་བར་ནི་བཞུགས་སུ་གསོལ།

Déshing yangpar bül lakna / Chi déwar ni shuk su söl //

As great as a billion worlds, these lotuses,
with eight petals and anthers, are lovely and vast.
I present them to you with one request:
choose the seat that best suits you and remain.

ཡན་ལག་བདུན་པ་ནི།
The Seven Branch Prayer

Seven Branch Prayers are excellent methods for accumulating merit through mind. It would be wonderful indeed if we could concretely produce the Buddhas, Bodhisattvas, pure realms, and offerings as described in the prayers, but it is also wonderful to produce them with a sincere mind. The Seven Branches are the most meritorious methods brought together and presented as one.

Concerning the branch of offerings, we should not imagine that the Buddhas are delighted with our offerings in a worldly way. They are delighted and rejoice because of our commitment to merit and enlightenment. Because Buddhas are the manifestation of compassion, the best offering we can make to them is our positive motivation and right-minded practice.

1) ཇི་སྙེད་སུ་དག་ཕྱོགས་བཅུའི་འཇིག་རྟེན་ན། དུས་གསུམ་གཤེགས་པ་མི་ཡི་
Jinyé sudak chok chu'i jikten na / Düsum shékpa miyi
སེང་གེ་ཀུན། བདག་གིས་མ་ལུས་དེ་དག་ཐམས་ཅད་ལ།
sengé kün / Dagi malu dédak tamché la /
ལུས་དང་ངག་ཡིད་དང་བས་ཕྱག་བགྱིའོ།
Lü tang ngayi tangwé chak gyi-o //

1) In all of the worlds in all ten directions
reside the Tathagathas, lions among men.
Before every one of them, without exception,
I bow down joyfully with body, speech, and mind.

2) བཟང་པོ་སྤྱོད་པའི་སྨོན་ལམ་སྟོབས་དག་གིས། རྒྱལ་བ་ཐམས་ཅད་
Zangpo chöpé mönlam tobdak gi / Gyalwa tamché
ཡིད་ཀྱིས་མངོན་སུམ་དུ། ཞིང་གི་རྡུལ་སྙེད་ལུས་རབ་བཏུད་པ་ཡིས།
yikyi ngön sum du / Shingi dülnyé lürab tüpa yi /
རྒྱལ་བ་ཀུན་ལ་རབ་ཏུ་ཕྱག་འཚལ་ལོ།
Gyalwa künla rabtu chak tsallo //

2) By the power of wishes of Excellent Conduct,
each Buddha evoked becomes manifest.
With as many bodies as atoms in the universe
I bow down deeply to the Victorious Ones.

3) རྡུལ་གཅིག་སྟེང་ན་རྡུལ་སྙེད་སངས་རྒྱས་རྣམས། སངས་རྒྱས་སྲས་ཀྱི་དབུས་ན་
Dül chik teng na dül nyé sangyé nam / Sangyé sékyi üna
བཞུགས་པ་དག དེ་ལྟར་ཆོས་ཀྱི་དབྱིངས་རྣམས་མ་ལུས་པར།
shukpa dak / Détar chökyi ying nam ma lü par /
ཐམས་ཅད་རྒྱལ་བ་དག་གིས་གང་བར་མོས།
Tamché gyalwa dagi kang war mö //

3) Buddhas, amidst countless Bodhisattvas,
crown each of the particles that has ever existed.
Thus Dharmadhatu, the entire sphere of being,
abounds with the Buddhas that I have envisioned.

4) དེ་དག་བསྔགས་པ་མི་ཟད་རྒྱ་མཚོ་རྣམས། དབྱངས་ཀྱི་ཡན་ལག་

Dédak ngakpa mizé gyatso nam / Yangi yenlak

རྒྱ་མཚོའི་སྒྲ་ཀུན་གྱིས། རྒྱལ་བ་ཀུན་གྱི་ཡོན་ཏན་རབ་བརྗོད་ཅིང་།

gyatso'i drakün gyi / Gyalwa kün gyi yönten rab jö shing /

བདེ་བར་གཤེགས་པ་ཐམས་ཅད་བདག་གིས་བསྟོད།

Déwar shékpa tamché da gi tö //

4) Using every tone of a multitude of melodies,
I revere them with boundless oceans of acclaim.
Singing the praises of Those Gone to Bliss,
I honor your qualities, O Victorious Ones.

5) མེ་ཏོག་དམ་པ་ཕྲེང་བ་དམ་པ་དང་། སིལ་སྙན་རྣམས་དང་

Métok dampa tréngwa dampa tang / Silnyen nam tang

བྱུག་པའི་གདུགས་མཆོག་དང་། མར་མེ་མཆོག་དང་བདུག་སྤོས་དམ་པ་ཡིས།

jukpé duk chok tang / Marmé chok tang dukpö dampa yi /

རྒྱལ་བ་དེ་དག་ལ་ནི་མཆོད་པར་བགྱི།

Gyalwa dédak lani chö par gyi //

5) Beautiful garlands, sumptuous flowers,
precious parasols, fine cymbals and balms,
radiant lamps, and the most fragrant incense:
I offer them to you, O Victorious Ones.

6) ན་བཟའ་དམ་པ་རྣམས་དང་དྲི་མཆོག་དང་། ཕྱེ་མའི་ཕུར་མ་
Naza dampa nam tang dri chok tang / Chémé purma
རི་རབ་མཉམ་པ་དང་། བཀོད་པ་ཁྱད་པར་འཕགས་པའི་མཆོག་ཀུན་གྱིས།
rirab nyampa tang / Köpa kyépar pakpé chok kün gyi /
རྒྱལ་བ་དེ་དག་ལ་ནི་མཆོད་པར་བགྱི།
Gyalwa dédak lani chö par gyi //

6) Such wonderful arrays, all perfectly presented:
exquisite apparel and sweet-smelling perfume,
jars of scented powder piled high like a mountain,
I offer them to you, O Victorious Ones.

7) མཆོད་པ་གང་རྣམས་བླ་མེད་རྒྱ་ཆེ་བ། དེ་དག་རྒྱལ་བ་
Chöpa kangnam lamé gya ché wa / Dédak gyalwa
ཐམས་ཅད་ལ་ཡང་མོས། བཟང་པོ་སྤྱོད་ལ་དད་པའི་སྟོབས་དག་གིས།
tamché la yang mö / Zangpo chöla dépé tobdak gi /
རྒྱལ་བ་ཀུན་ལ་ཕྱག་འཚལ་མཆོད་པར་བགྱི།
Gyalwa künla chaktsal chö par gyi //

7) Through these countless, superlative offerings,
I express my devotion to all of the Buddhas.
With the strength of conviction in Excellent Conduct,
I bow and present them to the Victorious Ones.

8) འདོད་ཆགས་ཞེ་སྡང་གཏི་མུག་དབང་གིས་ནི། ལུས་དང་ངག་དང་
Döchak shédang timuk wangi ni / Lü tang nga tang
དེ་བཞིན་ཡིད་ཀྱིས་ཀྱང་། སྡིག་པ་བདག་གིས་བགྱིས་པ་ཅི་མཆིས་པ།
déshin yikyi kyang / Dikpa dagi gyipa chichi pa /
དེ་དག་ཐམས་ཅད་བདག་གིས་སོ་སོར་བཤགས།
Dédak tamché dagi so sor shak //

8) Whatever misdeeds I may have committed
through body and speech, as well as through mind,
all outcomes of passion and anger and ignorance:
I openly disclose each and every one.

9) ཕྱོགས་བཅུའི་རྒྱལ་བ་ཀུན་དང་སངས་རྒྱས་སྲས། རང་རྒྱལ་རྣམས་དང་
Chok chu'i gyalwa kün tang sangyé sé / Rang gyal nam tang
སློབ་དང་མི་སློབ་དང་། འགྲོ་བ་ཀུན་གྱི་བསོད་ནམས་གང་ལ་ཡང་།
lob tang milob tang / Drowa kun gyi sönam kang la yang /
དེ་དག་ཀུན་གྱི་རྗེས་སུ་བདག་ཡི་རང་།
Dédak kün gyi jésu da yi rang //

9) I rejoice in each occurrence of merit produced
by Buddhas and Bodhisattvas of all ten directions,
by Pratyekabuddhas, by those training on the path,
by Arhats beyond training, and by every single being.

10) གང་རྣམས་ཕྱོགས་བཅུའི་འཇིག་རྟེན་སྒྲོན་མ་དག། བྱང་ཆུབ་རིམ་པར་
Kang nam chok chu'i jikten drönma dak / Jangchub rimpar
སངས་རྒྱས་མ་ཆགས་བརྙེས། མགོན་པོ་དེ་དག་བདག་གིས་ཐམས་ཅད་ལ།
sangyé ma chak nyé / Gönpo dédak dagi tamché la /
འཁོར་ལོ་བླ་ན་མེད་པར་བསྐོར་བར་བསྐུལ།
Khorlo lana mépar kor war kül //

10) O lanterns who illumine worlds in all ten directions,
by way of the progressive stages of awakening
you have become Buddhas, free from attachment.
Protectors, I entreat you all: turn the Supreme Wheel.

11) མྱ་ངན་འདའ་སྟོན་གང་བཞེད་དེ་དག་ལ། འགྲོ་བ་ཀུན་ལ་
Nya ngen datön kangshé dé dak la / Drowa kün la
ཕན་ཞིང་བདེ་བའི་ཕྱིར། བསྐལ་པ་ཞིང་གི་རྡུལ་སྙེད་བཞུགས་པར་ཡང་།
pen shing déwé chir / Kalpa shingi dül nyé shuk par yang /
བདག་གིས་ཐལ་མོ་རབ་སྦྱར་གསོལ་བར་བགྱི།
Dagi talmo rab jar söl war gyi //

11) Palms joined, I beseech those among you
who mean to manifest the state beyond suffering:
for as many eons as there are atoms in the universe,
remain for the welfare and happiness of all beings.

12) ཕྱག་འཚལ་བ་དང་མཆོད་ཅིང་བཤགས་པ་དང་། རྗེས་སུ་ཡི་རང་
Chak tsalwa tang chö shing shakpa tang / Jésu yirang
བསྐུལ་ཞིང་གསོལ་བ་ཡི། དགེ་བ་ཅུང་ཟད་བདག་གིས་ཅི་བསགས་པ།
külshing söl wa yi / Géwa chungzé dagi chi sakpa /
ཐམས་ཅད་བདག་གིས་བྱང་ཆུབ་ཕྱིར་བསྔོའོ།
Tamché dagi jangchub chir ngo-o //

12) Whatever small merit has been garnered here
through prostrating, offering, and confessing,
rejoicing, entreating, and beseeching,
I dedicate it all for the sake of enlightenment.

35 Buddhas Sutra: The Bodhisattva's Confession of Downfalls

Homage to the 35 Buddhas (Prostrations)

བྱང་ཆུབ་སེམས་དཔའི་ལྟུང་བ་བཤགས་པ་བཞུགས་སོ།
Homage to the 35 Buddhas (Prostrations)

While countless Buddha fields exist throughout our universe, Buddha Shakyamuni selected 35 Buddhas from 35 Buddha fields situated near our own solar system for this sutra. These Buddhas have a special karmic connection to our world. When we invoke them, we imagine that we are inviting them to come from their respective paradises in order to spend time in the pure realm that we have mentally created for them.

Because the wisdom of the Buddhas is limitless, if we supplicate them with genuine devotion they will be present everywhere. They instantaneously take their seats on the lotus thrones we present to them and naturally and spontaneously fulfill the positive wishes of all beings. Each Buddha is described as having his own characteristics and Buddha field, but it is not necessary to focus on these. While detailed explanations exist and can be very useful and inspiring for some practitioners, in general the main point is confidence and devotion. Correct attitude is truly the key.

Prostrations: Bowing Down Before the 35 Buddhas

In this section, we imagine that we bow down before the Buddhas while reciting their names. When accumulating prostrations for the preliminary practices or practicing together, we repeat the entire series of 35 names while physically doing the prostrations. In this case, the physical prostrations alone are counted; the number of recitations need not match the number of prostrations. During group practice, we do kneeling prostrations as we recite the names; during our personal practice we do full body prostrations. While prostrating, we visualize all sentient beings in precious human form and imagine that they join us as we practice.

see Appendix II for other recitation options

35 Buddha Names (Tibetan Version)

།སེམས་ཅན་ཐམས་ཅད་རྟག་པར་སངས་རྒྱས་ལ་སྐྱབས་སུ་མཆིའོ།
Semchen tamché takpar sangyé la kyab su chi-o /

།ཆོས་ལ་སྐྱབས་སུ་མཆིའོ། །དགེ་འདུན་ལ་སྐྱབས་སུ་མཆིའོ།
Chö la kyab su chi-o / Gendün la kyab su chi-o /

།བཅོམ་ལྡན་འདས་དེ་བཞིན་གཤེགས་པ་དགྲ་བཅོམ་པ་ཡང་དག་པར་
1) *Chomdendé déshin shékpa drachompa yangdakpar*
རྫོགས་པའི་སངས་རྒྱས་ཤཱཀྱ་ཐུབ་པ་ལ་ཕྱག་འཚལ་ལོ།
dzokpé sangyé shakya tubpa la chak tsallo /

།རྡོ་རྗེའི་སྙིང་པོས་རབ་ཏུ་འཇོམས་པ་ལ་ཕྱག་འཚལ་ལོ།
2) *Dorjé nyingpö rabtu jompa la chak tsallo /*

།རིན་ཆེན་འོད་འཕྲོ་ལ་ཕྱག་འཚལ་ལོ། །ཀླུ་དབང་གི་རྒྱལ་པོ་ལ་ཕྱག་འཚལ་ལོ།
3) *Rinchen ötro la chak tsallo /* 4) *Luwangi gyalpo la chak tsallo /*

།དཔའ་བོའི་སྡེ་ལ་ཕྱག་འཚལ་ལོ། །དཔལ་དགྱེས་ལ་ཕྱག་འཚལ་ལོ།
5) *Pawo'i dé la chak tsallo /* 6) *Palgyé la chak tsallo /*

།རིན་ཆེན་མེ་ལ་ཕྱག་འཚལ་ལོ། །རིན་ཆེན་ཟླ་འོད་ལ་ཕྱག་འཚལ་ལོ།
7) *Rinchen mé la chak tsallo /* 8) *Rinchen da ö la chak tsallo /*

།མཐོང་བ་དོན་ཡོད་ལ་ཕྱག་འཚལ་ལོ། །རིན་ཆེན་ཟླ་བ་ལ་ཕྱག་འཚལ་ལོ།
9) *Tongwa dönyö la chak tsallo /* 10) *Rinchen dawa la chak tsallo /*

།དྲི་མ་མེད་པ་ལ་ཕྱག་འཚལ་ལོ། །དཔལ་བྱིན་ལ་ཕྱག་འཚལ་ལོ།
11) Drima mépa la chak tsallo / 12) Paljin la chak tsallo /

།ཚངས་པ་ལ་ཕྱག་འཚལ་ལོ། །ཚངས་པས་བྱིན་ལ་ཕྱག་འཚལ་ལོ།
13) Tsangpa la chak tsallo / 14) Tsangpé jin la chak tsallo /

།ཆུ་ལྷ་ལ་ཕྱག་འཚལ་ལོ། །ཆུ་ལྷའི་ལྷ་ལ་ཕྱག་འཚལ་ལོ།
15) Chu lha la chak tsallo / 16) Chu lha'i lha la chak tsallo /

།དཔལ་བཟང་ལ་ཕྱག་འཚལ་ལོ། །ཙནྡན་དཔལ་ལ་ཕྱག་འཚལ་ལོ།
17) Palzang la chak tsallo / 18) Tsenden pal la chak tsallo /

།གཟི་བརྗིད་མཐའ་ཡས་ལ་ཕྱག་འཚལ་ལོ། །འོད་དཔལ་ལ་ཕྱག་འཚལ་ལོ།
19) Ziji tayé la chak tsallo / 20) Öpal la chak tsallo /

།མྱ་ངན་མེད་པའི་དཔལ་ལ་ཕྱག་འཚལ་ལོ། །སྲེད་མེད་ཀྱི་བུ་ལ་ཕྱག་འཚལ་ལོ།
21) Nya ngen mépé pal la chak tsallo / 22) Sémékyi bu la chak tsallo /

།མེ་ཏོག་དཔལ་ལ་ཕྱག་འཚལ་ལོ།
23) Métok pal la chak tsallo /

།དེ་བཞིན་གཤེགས་པ་ཚངས་པའི་འོད་ཟེར་རྣམ་པར་རོལ་པ་
24) Déshin shékpa tsangpé öser nampar rölpa

མངོན་པར་མཁྱེན་པ་ལ་ཕྱག་འཚལ་ལོ།
ngönpar kyenpa la chak tsallo /

།དེ་བཞིན་གཤེགས་པ་པདྨའི་འོད་ཟེར་རྣམ་པར་རོལ་པ་
25) Déshin shékpa pémé öser nampar rölpa

མངོན་པར་མཁྱེན་པ་ལ་ཕྱག་འཚལ་ལོ།
ngönpar kyenpa la chak tsallo /

།ནོར་དཔལ་ལ་ཕྱག་འཚལ་ལོ། །དྲན་པའི་དཔལ་ལ་ཕྱག་འཚལ་ལོ།
26) Norpal la chak tsallo / 27) Drenpé pal la chak tsallo /

།མཚན་དཔལ་ཤིན་ཏུ་ཡོངས་གྲགས་ལ་ཕྱག་འཚལ་ལོ།
28) Tsenpal shintu yongdrak la chak tsallo /

།དབང་པོའི་ཏོག་གི་རྒྱལ་མཚན་གྱི་རྒྱལ་པོ་ལ་ཕྱག་འཚལ་ལོ།
29) Wangpö toki gyaltsen gyi gyalpo la chak tsallo /

།ཤིན་ཏུ་རྣམ་པར་གནོན་པའི་དཔལ་ལ་ཕྱག་འཚལ་ལོ།
30) Shintu nampar nönpé pal la chak tsallo /

།གཡུལ་ལས་ཤིན་ཏུ་རྣམ་པར་རྒྱལ་བ་ལ་ཕྱག་འཚལ་ལོ།
31) Yüllé shintu nampar gyalwa la chak tsallo /

།རྣམ་པར་གནོན་པས་གཤེགས་པའི་དཔལ་ལ་ཕྱག་འཚལ་ལོ།
32) Nampar nönpé shékpé pal la chak tsallo /

།ཀུན་ནས་སྣང་བ་བཀོད་པའི་དཔལ་ལ་ཕྱག་འཚལ་ལོ།
33) Künné nangwa köpé pal la chak tsallo /

།རིན་ཆེན་པདྨ་རྣམ་པར་གནོན་པ་ལ་ཕྱག་འཚལ་ལོ།
34) Rinchen péma nampar nönpa la chak tsallo /

།དེ་བཞིན་གཤེགས་པ་དགྲ་བཅོམ་པ་ཡང་དག་པར་རྫོགས་པའི་

35) Déshin shékpa drachompa yangdakpar dzokpé

སངས་རྒྱས་རིན་པོ་ཆེ་དང་པདྨའི་གདན་ལ་

sangyé rinpoché tang pémé den la

རབ་ཏུ་བཞུགས་པ་རི་དབང་གི་རྒྱལ་པོ་ལ་ཕྱག་འཚལ་ལོ།

rabtu shukpa riwangi gyalpo la chak tsallo //

35 Buddha Names (Sanskrit Version)

1) Namo bhagavaté shakyamunayé
tathagatayarhaté samyak-sambuddhaya

2) Namo vajrasara pramardiné

3) Namo ratnarchishé

4) Namo nageshvara-rajaya

5) Namo virasenaya

6) Namo vira-nandiné

7) Namo ratnagnayé

8) Namo ratnachandraprabhaya

9) Namo amogha-darshiné

10) Namo ratna-chandraya

11) Namo nirmalaya

12) Namah shura-dattaya

13) Namo brahmané

14) Namo brahmadattaya

15) Namo varunaya

16) Namo varunadevaya

17) Namo bhadra-shriyé

18) Namash-chandana-shriyé

19) Namo anantau-jassé

20) Namah prabhasa-shriyé

21) Namo ashoka-shriyé

22) Namo narayanaya

23) Namah kusuma-shriyé

24) Namo brahma-jyotir-vikriditabhi-gnaya tathagataya

25) Namah padma-jyotir-vikriditabhi-gnaya tathagataya

26) Namo dhana-shriyé

27) Namah smriti-shriyé

28) Namah supari-kirtita-nama-dhéya-shriyé

29) Nama indra-kétud-vaja-rajaya

30) Namah suvikranta-shriyé

31) Namah suvijita-samgra-maya

32) Namo vikranta-gamishriyé

33) Namah samanta-vabhasa-vyuha-shriyé

34) Namo ratna-padma-vikraminé

35) Namo ratna-padma-supratishtita-shailendra-rajaya
tathagatayarhaté samyak-sambuddhaya

35 Buddha Names (English Version)

All sentient beings continuously take refuge in the Buddha, take refuge in the Dharma, take refuge in the Sangha.

1) I bow down before the Bhagavan, the Transcendent Victor, the Tathagatha Who Has Gone Thus, the Arhat who has Overcome All Foes, the Perfectly Authentic Buddha, Sage of the Shakyas.

2) I bow down before He Who Conquers All Through Vajra Essence.

3) I bow down before Jewel of Radiant Light.

4) I bow down before King of the Powerful Nagas.

5) I bow down before He of the Heroes.

6) I bow down before Joyful Glory.

7) I bow down before Jewel of Fire.

8) I bow down before Jewel of Moonlight.

9) I bow down before Meaningful to Behold.

10) I bow down before Jewel Moon.

11) I bow down before Immaculate One.

12) I bow down before Gift of Glory.

13) I bow down before The Pure One.

14) I bow down before Gift of the Pure One.

15) I bow down before God of the Water.

16) I bow down before God of Gods of the Water.

17) I bow down before Excellent Glory.

18) I bow down before Glorious Sandalwood.

19) I bow down before Infinite Splendor.

20) I bow down before Glorious Light.

21) I bow down before Glory Free from Torment.

22) I bow down before Son of No Desire.

23) I bow down before Glorious Flower.

24) I bow down before Buddha Light of the Pure One, Manifold Display of Manifest Clairvoyance.

25) I bow down before Buddha Light of the Lotus, Manifold Display of Manifest Clairvoyance.

26) I bow down before Wealth of Glory.

27) I bow down before Glory of Vigilance.

28) I bow down before Sign of Glory that Proclaims Throughout.

29) I bow down before King of the Royal Banner of the Pinnacle of Power.

30) I bow down before Glory Who Utterly Overcomes.

31) I bow down before Absolute Victor of Battles.

32) I bow down before Buddha Who Overcomes Completely.

33) I bow down before Glorious Array of All that Appears.

34) I bow down before Precious Lotus That Utterly Overcomes.

35) I bow down before the Tathagatha Who Has Gone Thus,
the Arhat who has Overcome All Foes,
the Perfectly Authentic Buddha, King of the Powerful Mountain
Who Abides Perfectly on a Seat of Jewel Lotus.

Mandala Offering

Mandala Offering Practice

མཎྜལ་འབུལ་བ་ནི།
Mandala Offering Practice

The mandala offering is the supreme method that sows seeds for rebirth in pure realms where we can continue our training as Bodhisattvas. From one lifetime to the next, we manifest in the best possible conditions until full enlightenment has been attained. In the opposite situation, beings who are reborn in the lower realms have no opportunity to put the Dharma into practice.

When we train in offering mandalas, we are replacing our impure universe with pure manifestation. We offer everything that is described in the text, from the most precious things that beings could possibly desire to divine paradises that encourage Buddhas to benefit beings. Because space is boundless, we can mentally fill it with our offerings to the Buddhas. In this case, we are the creators, and instead of creating worldly pleasures and fostering desire, we are creating excellent conditions that help Buddhas in their efforts to liberate beings.

If we have a mandala base, we wipe it clean of any dust as we recite the hundred syllable mantra, beginning with "Om Benza Sato..." With this, we imagine that all of the misdeeds and veils accumulated in the mindstreams of ourselves and others due to dualistic clinging have been completely purified.

Then, while visualizing the field of refuge (the Buddhas surrounded by Bodhisattvas, Pratyekabuddhas, Arhats, and so on), we perform the 37-point mandala offering, followed by the short verse beginning with "Sashi pöchü" ("This ground, sprinkled with perfumed water..."). We make heaps of flowers, rice, etc., and offer them as we recite the text, bearing in mind the meaning of the words.

Whether we are accumulating offerings or not, and whether our offering is extensive or abridged, we evoke the 37-point mandala visualization along with other splendid pure realms and imagine that we offer them all.

If we are accumulating 100,000 mandala offerings as a preliminary practice, each recitation of the short verse that begins "Sashi pöchü" ("This ground, sprinkled with perfumed water...") is counted. Detailed instructions should be received from a qualified teacher before we engage in the accumulations.

100 Syllable Mantra

ཨོཾ་བཛྲ་ས་ཏྭ་ས་མ་ཡ། མ་ནུ་པཱ་ལ་ཡ། བཛྲ་ས་ཏྭ་ཏྭེ་ནོ་པ་ཏིཥྛ་དྲི་ཌྷོ་མེ་བྷ་ཝ།
སུ་ཏོ་ཥྱོ་མེ་བྷ་ཝ། སུ་པོ་ཥྱོ་མེ་བྷ་ཝ། ཨ་ནུ་རཀྟོ་མེ་བྷ་ཝ། སརྦ་སིདྡྷི་མྨེ་པྲ་ཡཙྪ།
སརྦ་ཀརྨ་སུ་ཙ་མེ་ཙིཏྟཾ་ཤྲི་ཡཿ ཀུ་རུ་ཧཱུྃ་ཧ་ཧ་ཧ་ཧ་ཧོཿ བྷ་ག་ཝཱན།
སརྦ་ཏ་ཐཱ་ག་ཏ་བཛྲ་མཱ་མེ་མུཉྩ་བཛྲཱི་བྷ་ཝ་མ་ཧཱ་ས་མ་ཡ་ས་ཏྭ་ཨཱཿ

Om benza satto samaya / manu palaya / benza satto té nopa tishta drido mé bhava / suto kayo mé bhava / supo kayo mé bhava / anu rakto mé bhava / sarva siddhi mémtra yatsa / sarva karma sutsamé tsitam chirya kuru hung / ha ha ha ha ho bhagavan / sarva tathagata benza mamé muntsa benzi bhava maha samaya satto ah //

ཨོཾ་བཛྲ་བྷཱུ་མི་ཨཱཿཧཱུྃ།

Om benza bhumi ah hung

གཞི་རྣམ་པར་དག་པ་དབང་ཆེན་གསེར་གྱི་ས་གཞི།

Shi nampar dakpa wangchen sérgyi sa shi /

The pure foundation is the mighty golden ground.

ཨོཾ་བཛྲ་རེ་ཁེ་ཨཱཿཧཱུྃ།

Om benza rékhé ah hung

ཕྱི་ལྕགས་རིའི་འཁོར་ཡུག་གི་ར་བས་ཡོངས་སུ་བསྐོར་བའི་

Chi chak ri'i khor yuki rawé yongsu korwé

དབུས་སུ་རིའི་རྒྱལ་པོ་རི་བོ་མཆོག་རབ།

üsu ri'i gyalpo riwo chok rab //

The outer rim is encircled by a ring of iron mountains.

ཤར་ལུས་འཕགས་པོ། ལྷོ་འཛམ་བུ་གླིང་། ནུབ་བ་ལང་སྤྱོད།

Shar lüpapo / lho dzambuling / nub balang chö /

བྱང་སྒྲ་མི་སྙན། ལུས་དང་ལུས་འཕགས། རྔ་ཡབ་དང་རྔ་ཡབ་གཞན།

jang dra mi nyen / lü tang lü pak / nga yab tang nga yab shen /

གཡོ་ལྡན་དང་ལམ་མཆོག་འགྲོ། སྒྲ་མི་སྙན་དང་སྒྲ་མི་སྙན་གྱི་ཟླ།

yo den tang lam chok dro / dra mi nyen tang dra mi nyen gyi da /

In the center is Meru, King of Mountains. Purvavideha is in the east, Jambudvipa is in the south, Aparagodaniya is in the west, Uttarakuru is in the north. Beside them are Deha and Videha; Camara and Aparacamara; Shatha and Uttaramantrina; Kurava and Kaurava.

རིན་པོ་ཆེའི་རི་བོ། དཔག་བསམ་གྱི་ཤིང་། འདོད་འཇོའི་བ། མ་རྨོས་པའི་ལོ་ཏོག

Rinpoché'i riwo / paksam gyi shing / dö jo'i ba / mamö pa'i lotok /

འཁོར་ལོ་རིན་པོ་ཆེ། ནོར་བུ་རིན་པོ་ཆེ། བཙུན་མོ་རིན་པོ་ཆེ།

Khorlo rinpoché / norbu rinpoché / tsünmo rinpoché /

བློན་པོ་རིན་པོ་ཆེ། གླང་པོ་རིན་པོ་ཆེ། རྟ་མཆོག་རིན་པོ་ཆེ།

lönpo rinpoché / langpo rinpoché / tachok rinpoché /

དམག་དཔོན་རིན་པོ་ཆེ། གཏེར་ཆེན་པོའི་བུམ་པ། སྒེག་མོ་མ། ཕྲེང་བ་མ།

makpön rinpoché / térchenpo'i bumpa / gékmoma / tréngwama /

གླུ་མ། གར་མ། མེ་ཏོག་མ། བདུག་སྤོས་མ། སྣང་གསལ་མ།

luma / garma / métokma / dukpöma / nang salma /

དྲི་ཆབ་མ། ཉི་མ། ཟླ་བ། རིན་པོ་ཆེའི་གདུགས། ཕྱོགས་ལས་རྣམ་པར་

dri chabma / nyima / dawa / rinpoché'i duk / Cholé nampar

རྒྱལ་བའི་རྒྱལ་མཚན། དབུས་སུ་ལྷ་དང་མིའི་དཔལ་འབྱོར་ཕུན་སུམ་

gyalwé gyaltsen / üsu lha tang mi'i paljor pünsum

ཚོགས་པ་མ་ཚང་བ་མེད་པ།

tsok pa ma tsangwa mé pa /

རབ་འབྱམས་རྒྱ་མཚོའི་རྡུལ་གྱི་གྲངས་ལས་འདས་པ་མངོན་པར་བཀོད་དེ།

rabjam gyatso'i dul gyi drang lé dépa ngönpar kö dé //

There are the jewel mountain; the wish-fulfilling tree; the bountiful cow; the effortless harvest; the precious wheel; the precious gem; the precious queen; the precious minister; the precious elephant; the fine and precious horse; the precious general; the great treasure vase; the goddess of grace; the goddess of garlands; the goddess of song; the goddess of dance; the goddess of flowers; the goddess of incense; the goddess of light; the goddess of perfume; the sun; the moon; the precious parasol; the royal banner that triumphs in all directions. In the center is the most plentiful wealth of gods and humans: nothing is lacking. Even more abundant than the atoms of the boundless oceans, everything becomes manifest and is clearly displayed.

བཅོམ་ལྡན་འདས་དེ་བཞིན་གཤེགས་པ་དགྲ་བཅོམ་པ་ཡང་དག་པར་རྫོགས་པའི་སངས་རྒྱས་

Chomdendé déshin shékpa drachompa yangdakpar dzokpé sangyé

གསུམ་བཅུ་རྩ་ལྔ་དང་། གཞན་ཡང་ཕྱོགས་བཅུའི་འཇིག་རྟེན་གྱི་ཁམས་ཐམས་ཅད་ན་

sum chu so nga tang / shen yang chok chu'i jikten gyi kham tamché na

བཞུགས་པའི་སངས་རྒྱས་དང་འཁོར་ཉན་རང་བྱང་སེམས་དང་བཅས་པ་རྣམས་ལ་

shukpé sangyé tang khor / nyan rang jangsem tang chépa nam la

འབུལ་བར་བགྱིའོ། ཐུགས་རྗེས་འགྲོ་བའི་དོན་དུ་བཞེས་སུ་གསོལ།

bülwar gyi-o / tukjé drowé döndu shé su söl /

བཞེས་ནས་བྱིན་གྱིས་བརླབ་ཏུ་གསོལ།

shéné jin gyi lab tu söl //

I offer it to the Bhagavans, the Tathagathas, the Arhats, the 35 utterly perfect Buddhas, as well as to the Buddhas residing in all of the worlds in all ten directions with their retinues of Shravakas, Pratyekabuddhas, and Bodhisattvas. Please accept it with compassion for the benefit of beings; and having accepted it, please grant your blessings.

When accumulating mandala offerings,
repeat and count the following lines:

ས་གཞི་སྤོས་ཆུས་བྱུགས་ཤིང་མེ་ཏོག་བཀྲམ། རི་རབ་གླིང་བཞི་ཉི་ཟླས་
Sashi pöchü juk shing métok tram / rirab ling shi nyidé

བརྒྱན་པ་འདི། སངས་རྒྱས་ཞིང་དུ་དམིགས་ཏེ་ཕུལ་བ་ཡིས།
gyen pa di / sangyé shing du mikté pülwa yi /

འགྲོ་ཀུན་རྣམ་དག་ཞིང་ལ་སྤྱོད་པར་ཤོག།
drokün namdak shing la chöpar sho //

This ground, sprinkled with perfumed water,
strewn with flowers, adorned with Mount Meru,
the four continents, the sun, and the moon:
I imagine it as a Buddha-field and offer it
so that all beings may experience the pure realms.

ཞེས་ཚར་ཅི་ནུས་སུ་འབུལ་ལ་རྗེས་སུ།
Make this offering as many times as you can. After that...

ཕྱོགས་བཅུ་དུས་གསུམ་བཞུགས་པ་ཡི། སངས་རྒྱས་བྱང་ཆུབ་སེམས་དཔའ་དང་།
Chok chu düsum shuk pa yi / sangyé jangchub sempa tang /

ཉན་ཐོས་རང་རྒྱལ་དགྲ་བཅོམ་ཚོགས། དུས་གསུམ་བདེ་གཤེགས་མ་ལུས་ལ།
nyentö rang gyal drachom tsok / düsum déshék ma lu la /

གླིང་བཞི་རི་རབ་བཅས་པ་དང་། གླིང་བཞི་བྱེ་བ་ཕྲག་བརྒྱ་དང་།
ling shi rirab chépa tang / ling shi jéwa trak gya tang /

བྱེ་བ་འབུམ་དང་དུང་ཕྱུར་ཏེ། མཎྜལ་གཅིག་ཏུ་བསྡུས་ནས་ནི།
jéwa bum tang dung jor té / mandal chiktu düné ni/

མོས་བློས་གོང་མ་རྣམས་ལ་འབུལ། ཐུགས་རྗེས་བརྩེར་དགོངས་བཞེས་སུ་གསོལ།

mölö gongma nam la bul / tukjé tsérgong shé su söl /

གཞེས་ནས་བྱིན་གྱིས་བརླབ་ཏུ་གསོལ།

shéné jingyi lab tu söl //

O Buddhas and Bodhisattvas of the three times and ten directions,
Assembly of Shravakas, Pratyekabuddhas and Arhats,
past, present and future Sugatas, without exception:

the four continents, with Mount Meru, a billion times the four continents, a hundred million and a thousand billion, are gathered together in this one mandala -

I offer it to you, superior ones, with veneration.
Through your compassion, consider it with love and accept it, and having consented, please grant your blessings.

ཨོཾ་མཎྜལ་པཱུཛ་མེགྷ་ས་མུ་དྲ་ས་ཕ་ར་ཎ་ས་མ་ཡེ་ཨཱཿཧཱུྃ།

Om mandala pudza mégha samudra saparana samayé ah hung

མཉེས་བྱེད་མཎྜལ་བཟང་པོ་འདི་ཕུལ་བས། བྱང་ཆུབ་ལམ་ལ་བར་ཆད་
Nyéjé mandal zangpo di pulwé / jangchub lamla barché

མི་འབྱུང་ཞིང་། དུས་གསུམ་བདེ་གཤེགས་དགོངས་པ་རྟོགས་པ་དང་། སྲིད་པར་མི་འཁྲུལ་
mi jung shing / düsum dérshék gongpa tokpa tang / sipar mitrül

ཞི་བར་མི་གནས་ཤིང་། ནམ་མཁའ་མཉམ་པའི་འགྲོ་བ་སྒྲོལ་བར་ཤོག།
shiwar mi né shing / namkha nyampé drowa drölwar sho //

By offering this excellent, pleasing mandala
may no obstacles arise on the path to enlightenment.
Neither remaining astray in samsara nor abiding in nirvana,
may I realize the wisdom mind of the Buddhas of the three times,
and may beings as numerous as the sky is vast be liberated.

35 Buddhas Sutra: The Bodhisattva's Confession of Downfalls

Confession

After the mandala offering, we continue with the main sutra, reciting it in full until the end.

དེ་དག་ལ་སོགས་པ་ཕྱོགས་བཅུའི་འཇིག་རྟེན་གྱི་ཁམས་ཐམས་ཅད་ན་དེ་བཞིན་
Dédak la sokpa chok chu'i jikten gyi kham tamché na déshin
གཤེགས་པ་དགྲ་བཅོམ་པ་ཡང་དག་པར་རྫོགས་པའི་སངས་རྒྱས་བཅོམ་ལྡན་འདས་
shékpa drachompa yangdakpar dzokpé sangyé chomdendé
གང་ཇི་སྙེད་ཅིག་བཞུགས་ཏེ་འཚོ་ཞིང་བཞེས་པའི་སངས་རྒྱས་བཅོམ་ལྡན་འདས་
gang jinyé chik shukté / tso shing shépé sangyé chomdendé
དེ་དག་ཐམས་ཅད་བདག་ལ་དགོངས་སུ་གསོལ།
dédak tamché dala gong su söl //

O Tathagathas, Arhats, Utterly Perfect Buddhas, and Bhagavans;
all of you and more, in all of the worlds of all ten directions;
you Victorious Buddhas who abide here
to nurture, sustain, and watch over us:
all of you, please heed me!

བདག་གི་སྐྱེ་བ་འདི་དང་སྐྱེ་བ་ཐོག་མ་དང་མཐའ་མ་མ་མཆིས་པ་ནས།
Dagi kyéwa di tang kyéwa tokma tang tama machipa né /
འཁོར་བ་ན་འཁོར་བའི་སྐྱེ་གནས་ཐམས་ཅད་དུ་སྡིག་པའི་ལས་བགྱིས་པ་དང་།
khorwa na khorwé kyé né tamché du dikpé lé gyipa tang /
བགྱིད་དུ་སྩལ་བ་དང་། བགྱིས་པ་ལ་རྗེས་སུ་ཡི་རང་བའམ།
gyidu tsalwa tang / gyipa la jésu yi rang wa'am /

In this life and in beginningless and limitless lifetimes,
in all life situations within samsara, the cycle of existence,
I have done evil deeds, have made others do them,
and have rejoiced when they were done.

།མཆོད་རྟེན་གྱི་དཀོར་རམ། དགེ་འདུན་གྱི་དཀོར་རམ།
Chöten gyi korram / gendün gyi korram /
ཕྱོགས་བཅུའི་དགེ་འདུན་གྱི་དཀོར་ཕྲོགས་པ་དང་། འཕྲོག་ཏུ་སྩལ་བ་དང་།
chok chu'i gendün gyi kor trokpa tang / trok tu tsalwa tang /
འཕྲོག་པ་ལ་རྗེས་སུ་ཡི་རང་བའམ།
trokpa la jésu yi rang wa'am /

I have stolen that which is used for worship,
the belongings of Dharma communities, the belongings of Dharma communities of the ten directions; I have made others steal them, and have rejoiced when they were stolen.

མཚམས་མ་མཆིས་པ་ལྔའི་ལས་བགྱིས་པ་དང་། བགྱིད་དུ་སྩལ་བ་དང་།
Tsam machipa nga'i lé gyipa tang / gyidu tsalwa tang /
བགྱིས་པ་ལ་རྗེས་སུ་ཡི་རང་བའམ། མི་དགེ་བ་བཅུའི་ལས་ཀྱི་ལམ་ཡང་དག་པར་
gyipa la jésu yi rang wa'am / mi géwa chu'i lé kyi lam yangdakpar
བླངས་པ་ལ་ཞུགས་པ་དང་། འཇུག་ཏུ་སྩལ་བ་དང་།
langpa la shukpa tang / juktu tsalwa tang /
འཇུག་པ་ལ་རྗེས་སུ་ཡི་རང་བའམ།
jukpa la jésu yi rang wa'am /

I have committed the five limitless actions, have made others commit them, have rejoiced when they were committed . I have wholeheartedly taken the path of the ten non-virtuous actions, have made others take it, and have rejoiced when it was taken.

ལས་ཀྱི་སྒྲིབ་པ་གང་གིས་བསྒྲིབས་ནས། བདག་སེམས་ཅན་དམྱལ་བར་མཆི་བའམ།
Lékyi dribpa gangi drib né / da semchen nyalwar chi wa'am /

དུད་འགྲོའི་སྐྱེ་གནས་སུ་མཆི་བའམ། ཡི་དྭགས་ཀྱི་ཡུལ་དུ་མཆི་བའམ།
dündro'i kyé né su chi wa'am / yidak kyi yül du chi wa'am /

ཡུལ་མཐའ་འཁོབ་ཏུ་སྐྱེ་བའམ། ཀླ་ཀློར་སྐྱེ་བའམ། ལྷ་ཚེ་རིང་པོ་
yül ta khob tu kyé wa'am / lalor kyé wa'am / lha tséringpo

རྣམས་སུ་སྐྱེ་བའམ། དབང་པོ་མ་ཚང་བར་འགྱུར་བའམ།
nam su kyé wa'am / wangpo ma tsangwar gyur wa'am /

ལྟ་བ་ལོག་པར་འཛིན་པར་འགྱུར་བའམ།
tawa lokpar dzinpar gyur wa'am /

སངས་རྒྱས་འབྱུང་བ་ལ་མཉེས་པར་མི་བགྱིད་པར་འགྱུར་བའི་
sangyé jungwa la nyépar mi gyipar gyurwé

ལས་ཀྱི་སྒྲིབ་པ་གང་ལགས་པ།
lé kyi dribpa gang lakpa //

Once obscured by these karmic veils, whatever they may be, sentient beings and I myself will move on to the hell realms, to the animal realms, to the land of the hungry ghosts. I will be born in forsaken hinterlands, among barbarians, among the long-lived gods. I will have incomplete faculties, adhere to wrong views, disdain the advent of a Buddha.

དེ་དག་ཐམས་ཅད་སངས་རྒྱས་བཅོམ་ལྡན་འདས་ཡེ་ཤེས་སུ་གྱུར་པ།
Dédak tamché sangyé chomdendé yéshé su gyurpa /

སྤྱན་དུ་གྱུར་པ། དཔང་དུ་གྱུར་པ།
chen du gyurpa / pang du gyurpa /

ཚད་མར་གྱུར་པ། མཁྱེན་པ། གཟིགས་པ། དེ་དག་གི་སྤྱན་སྔར་མཐོལ་ལོ་འཆགས་སོ།
tsémar gyurpa / khyen pa / zik pa / dédak gi chen ngar töl lo chak so /

མི་འཆབ་བོ། །མི་སྦེད་དོ། སླན་ཆད་ཀྱང་གཅོད་ཅིང་སྡོམ་པར་བགྱིད་ལགས་སོ།
mi chab bo / mi bé do / lenché kyang chö shing dompar gyi lak so /

These karmic veils, whatever they may be, I acknowledge and confess them all in the presence of the Buddhas, the Victorious Ones, the Wise, the Eyes, the Witnesses, The Truthful, the Knowing, the Seeing.
I disclose them without concealing, without hiding.
I vow to refrain from committing them from this moment on.

Dedication

སངས་རྒྱས་བཅོམ་ལྡན་འདས་དེ་དག་ཐམས་ཅད་བདག་ལ་དགོངས་སུ་གསོལ།
Sangyé chomdendé dédak tamché da la gong su söl /

བདག་གིས་སྐྱེ་བ་འདི་དང་སྐྱེ་བ་ཐོག་མ་དང་མཐའ་མ་མ་མཆིས་པ་ནས།
Dagi kyéwa di tang kyéwa tokma tang tama ma chipa né /

འཁོར་བ་ན་འཁོར་བའི་སྐྱེ་གནས་གཞན་དག་ཏུ་སྦྱིན་པ་ཐ་ན་དུད་འགྲོའི་སྐྱེ་གནས་སུ་
Khorwa na khorwé kyé né shendak tu jinpa tana dündro'i kyé né su

སྐྱེས་པ་ལ་ཟས་ཁམ་གཅིག་ཙམ་བསྩལ་བའི་དགེ་བའི་རྩ་བ་གང་ལགས་པ་དང་།
kyépa la / zé kham chik tsam tsalwé géwé tsawa gang lakpa tang /

བདག་གིས་ཚུལ་ཁྲིམས་བསྲུངས་པའི་དགེ་བའི་རྩ་བ་གང་ལགས་པ་དང་།
Dagi tsültrim sungpé géwé tsawa gang lakpa tang /

བདག་གིས་ཚངས་པར་སྤྱོད་པ་ལ་གནས་པའི་དགེ་བའི་རྩ་བ་གང་ལགས་པ་དང་།
dagi tsangpar chöpa la népé géwé tsawa gang lakpa tang /

བདག་གིས་སེམས་ཅན་ཡོངས་སུ་སྨིན་པར་བགྱིས་པའི་དགེ་བའི་རྩ་བ་གང་ལགས་པ་དང་།
dagi semchen yongsu minpar gyipé géwé tsawa gang lakpa tang /

བདག་གིས་བྱང་ཆུབ་མཆོག་ཏུ་སེམས་བསྐྱེད་པའི་དགེ་བའི་རྩ་བ་གང་ལགས་པ་དང་།
dagi jangchub choktu sem kyépé géwé tsawa gang lakpa tang /

བདག་གིས་བླ་ན་མེད་པའི་ཡེ་ཤེས་ཀྱི་དགེ་བའི་རྩ་བ་གང་ལགས་པ་དེ་དག
dagi lana mépé yéshé kyi géwé tsawa gang lakpa dédak

ཐམས་ཅད་གཅིག་ཏུ་བསྡུས་ཤིང་བསྡུམས་ཏེ། བསྡོམས་ནས་བླ་ན་མ་མཆིས་པ་དང་།
tamché chiktu dü shing dum té / Dom né lana ma chipa tang /

གོང་ན་མ་མཆིས་པ་དང་། གོང་མའི་ཡང་གོང་མ་བླ་མའི་ཡང་བླ་མར་
gong na ma chipa tang / gong mé yang gong ma / lamé yang lamar

ཡོངས་སུ་བསྔོ་བས། བླ་ན་མེད་པ་ཡང་དག་པར་རྫོགས་པའི་

yong su ngowé / lana mépa yangdakpar dzokpé

བྱང་ཆུབ་ཏུ་ཡོངས་སུ་བསྔོ་བར་བགྱིའོ།

jangchub tu yong su ngowar gyi-o//

O Buddhas, Triumphant Ones, all of you: please heed me!
All roots of virtue that have resulted from the least act of generosity
in this life and in beginningless, limitless lifetimes,
in all life situations within samsara, the cycle of existence
—even if only through giving a scrap of food to an animal—
and those roots of virtue that exist because I have
maintained moral discipline,
and those that exist because I have sustained a pure lifestyle,
and those that exist because I have caused beings
to become spiritually mature,
and those that exist because I have developed supreme Bodhicitta,
and all those that exist because of the paramount wisdom within me,
I collect them into one, combine them,
bind them together, and dedicate them completely
to the higher than the highest, the greater than the greatest:
I dedicate them to unsurpassable, absolute, fully accomplished,
supreme enlightenment.

།ཇི་ལྟར་འདས་པའི་སངས་རྒྱས་བཅོམ་ལྡན་འདས་རྣམས་ཀྱིས་ཡོངས་སུ་བསྔོས་པ་དང་།
Jitar dépé sangyé chomdendé namkyi yong su ngöpa tang /
ཇི་ལྟར་མ་བྱོན་པའི་སངས་རྒྱས་བཅོམ་ལྡན་འདས་རྣམས་ཀྱིས་
Jitar ma jönpé sangyé chomdendé namkyi
ཡོངས་སུ་བསྔོ་བར་འགྱུར་བ་དང་།
yong su ngowar gyurwa tang/
ཇི་ལྟར་ད་ལྟར་བྱུང་བའི་སངས་རྒྱས་བཅོམ་ལྡན་འདས་རྣམས་ཀྱིས་
jitar datar jungwé sangyé chomdendé namkyi
ཡོངས་སུ་སྔོ་བར་མཛད་པ་དེ་བཞིན་དུ་བདག་གིས་ཀྱང་ཡོངས་སུ་བསྔོ་བར་བགྱིའོ།
yong su ngowar dzépa dé shindu dagi kyang yongsu ngo war gyi-o //

Just as the Bhagavan Buddhas of the past have dedicated completely, just as the Bhagavan Buddhas of the future will dedicate completely, just as the Bhagavan Buddhas who manifest in the present dedicate completely, in just the same way, I too dedicate completely.

།སྡིག་པ་ཐམས་ཅད་ནི་སོ་སོར་བཤགས་སོ། བསོད་ནམས་ཐམས་ཅད་ལ་རྗེས་སུ་
Dikpa tamché ni so sor shak so / sönam tamché la jésu
ཡི་རང་ངོ། སངས་རྒྱས་ཐམས་ཅད་ལ་བསྐུལ་ཞིང་གསོལ་བ་འདེབས་སོ།
yi rang ngo / sangyé tamché la kül shing sölwa deb so /
བདག་གིས་བླ་ན་མེད་པ་ཡེ་ཤེས་ཀྱི་མཆོག་དམ་པ་ཐོབ་པར་གྱུར་ཅིག།
dagi lana mépa yéshé kyi chok dampa tobpar gyur chik //

I confess each and every negative deed;
I rejoice in the whole of merit.
I entreat and beseech all of the Buddhas:
may I attain the supreme, true state of paramount wisdom.

།མི་མཆོག་རྒྱལ་བ་གང་དག་ད་ལྟར་བཞུགས་པ་དང་། གང་དག་འདས་པ་
Mi chok gyalwa gangdak datar shukpa tang / gangdak dépa
དག་དང་དེ་བཞིན་གང་མ་བྱོན། ཡོན་ཏན་བསྔགས་པ་མཐའ་ཡས་རྒྱ་མཚོ་
dak tang déshin gang ma jön / yönten ngakpa tayé gyatso
འདྲ་ཀུན་ལ། ཐལ་མོ་སྦྱར་བར་བགྱིས་ཏེ་སྐྱབས་སུ་ཉེ་བར་མཆིའོ།
dra kün la / talmo jarwar gyi té kyab su nyéwar chi-o //

Exalted Buddhas, kings among humans,
Buddhas who dwell in the present,
Buddhas of the past, and Buddhas yet to come,
you Buddhas who are like an infinite ocean of praiseworthy qualities:
my palms joined in prayer, I sincerely take refuge in all of you.

Concluding Prayers

Bodhisattva Vow

Requesting Clemency

Request to Depart and Return

Dedication of Merit

Wishing Prayers

Wish for Good Fortune

བྱང་ཆུབ་སེམས་པའི་སྡོམ་པ།
Bodhisattva Vow

Here again we are repeating our motivation to attain enlightenment for the benefit of all beings. The Bodhisattva vow, our commitment, is the seed of enlightenment. It is formulated in front of the Buddhas, the perfect witnesses.

In order to truly be capable of liberating beings, we must become qualified Bodhisattvas, and in order to accomplish the Bodhisattvas' wishes for beings, we must attain perfect enlightenment. The Bodhisattva vow states the Bodhisattva aspiration and lays out the path.

ཇི་ལྟར་སྔོན་གྱི་བདེ་གཤེགས་ཀྱིས། བྱང་ཆུབ་ཐུགས་ནི་བསྐྱེད་པ་དང་།
Jitar ngön gyi déshék kyi / jangchub tukni kyépa tang /

བྱང་ཆུབ་སེམས་པའི་བསླབ་པ་ལ། དེ་དག་རིམ་བཞིན་གནས་པ་ལྟར།
jangchub sempé lab pa la / dédak rimshin né pa tar /

དེ་བཞིན་འགྲོ་ལ་ཕན་དོན་དུ། བྱང་ཆུབ་སེམས་ནི་བསྐྱེད་བགྱི་ཞིང་།
déshin drola pen dön du / jangchub semni kyé gyi shing /

དེ་བཞིན་དུ་འཇུག་པའི་བསླབ་པ་ལ། རིམ་པ་བཞིན་དུ་བསླབ་པར་བགྱི།
dé shindu jukpé lab pa la / rimpa shindu labpar gyi //

Just as the Buddhas of the past developed enlightened mind
and progressively trained as Bodhisattvas,
I too will develop enlightened mind,
and train progressively in order to help beings.

ཞེས་ལན་གསུམ།
Repeat 3 times

བཟོད་གསོལ་ནི།
Requesting Clemency

The request for clemency is quite straightforward. In worldly situations, if we ask honored guests to forgive us for any mistakes or awkwardness, there may be a self-centered aspect to our request. Perhaps our motivation is to ensure the favors of our guests for a future project. Here our goal is entirely different. We sincerely ask forgiveness for any inconvenience, shortcomings, or errors, and vow to do our best to practice correctly in the future.

བདག་ཅག་དུས་ངན་པའི་སེམས་ཅན་སྤྱོད་པ་དམན་ཞིང་མ་དག་པས་
Dachak dü nganpé semchen chöpa men shing madakpé

འཚལ་བ་དང་། ལུས་ངག་ཡིད་གསུམ་ཉོན་མོངས་པ་དང་འདྲེས་པ་དང་
tsalwa tang / lü nga yi sum nyönmongpa tang drépa tang

མཆོད་པའི་དངོས་པོ་ཆུང་ཞིང་དམན་པ་དང་། གཙང་སྦྲས་མ་བྱེད་པ་དང་།
chöpé ngöpo chung shing menpa tang / tsangdré ma chépa tang /

མདོ་ལས་བྱུང་བའི་ཆོ་ག་བཞིན་དུ་མ་ཆོགས་པ་ལ་སོགས་པ་
dolé jungwé choka shindu ma chokpa la sokpa

འཁྲུལ་ཞིང་ནོངས་པ་ཐམས་ཅད་འཕགས་པ་ཐུགས་རྗེ་ཆེན་པོ་དང་
trul shing nongpa tamché pakpa tukjé chenpo tang

ལྡན་པ་རྣམས་ལ་བཟོད་པར་གསོལ་ཞིང་མཆིས་ན། ཐུགས་བརྩེ་བར་
denpa nam la zöpar söl shing chi na / tuk tséwar

དགོངས་ཏེ་བཟོད་པར་བཞེས་ཤིང་ཕྲལ་དང་ཡུན་དུ་བདག་ཅག་གི་སྒྲིབ་པར་
gong té zöpar shéshing drel tang yundu dachaki dripar

མི་འགྱུར་བར་བྱིན་གྱིས་བརླབ་ཏུ་གསོལ།
migyur war jingyi lab tu söl //

We beings of these decadent times have practiced in an inferior, impure way. Our body, speech, and mind were mixed with disturbing emotions; our offerings were meager and of inferior quality; we neglected purification; we were unable to properly carry out the Sutra ritual, and more.

O Noble Ones of Great Compassion,
we request your clemency for all confusion and errors.
Please look upon us with loving kindness, bear with us and grant us your blessing, that we may be free from such obscurations now and forevermore.

གཤེགས་གསོལ་ནི།
Request to Depart and Return

If our collective karma were pure enough, we could invite the Buddhas, and they would actually appear here in this world. But since we lack this merit, they can only appear to us in our minds. Now, in the same way as we see honored guests off as they leave for home, we respectfully send the Buddhas back to their respective pure lands and ask them to please come again when invited. The effect of the merit accumulated through sending off and inviting is that we will be reborn in worlds where Buddhas appear and will have the good fortune of being their disciples until we too reach enlightenment.

མགོན་པོ་ཐུགས་རྗེ་ཆེན་པོ་དང་ལྡན་པ་ཁྱེད་རྣམས་ཀྱིས་བདག་ཅག་
Gönpo tukjé chenpo tangdenpa kyénam kyi dachak

དང་སེམས་ཅན་ཐམས་ཅད་ཀྱི་དོན་མཛད་ལགས་ཀྱི་སོ་སོའི་ཞིང་ཁམས་སུ་
tang semchen tamché kyi döndzé lakyi so so'i shingkham su

འཁོར་དང་བཅས་པ་གཤེགས་སུ་གསོལ་ལ།
khor tangchépa shék su söl la /

སླར་ཡང་སེམས་ཅན་གྱི་དོན་ལ་ཐུགས་རྗེས་འབྱོན་པར་ཞུ།
Laryang semchen gyi dön la tukjé jönpar shu //

Lords, Protectors, Great Compassionate Ones,
you who act for our welfare and that of all beings:
with your entourage, please go now to your chosen Pure Land.
We ask you: kindly come back again in order to benefit beings.

བསྔོ་བ་ནི། Dedication of Merit

In these standard dedication and wishing prayers we state our motivation to liberate all beings through the positive spiritual energy garnered through our practice. We then formulate the prayer that all beings may one day have the perfect qualities of the Buddha.

བསོད་ནམས་འདི་ཡིས་ཐམས་ཅད་གཟིགས་པ་ཉིད།
Sönam diyi tamché zikpa nyi /
ཐོབ་ནས་ཉེས་པའི་དགྲ་རྣམས་ཕམ་བྱས་ནས།
Tobné nyépé dranam pam jé né/
སྐྱེ་རྒ་ན་འཆིའི་རྦ་རླབས་འཁྲུགས་པ་ཡི།
kyé ga na chi'i balab truk pa yi/
སྲིད་པའི་མཚོ་ལས་འགྲོ་བ་སྒྲོལ་བར་ཤོག།
sipé tsolé drowa drölwar sho //

Through this merit may I attain true omniscience .
Then, having defeated all adversaries,
may I liberate beings from the ocean of existence
and its turbulent waves of birth, old age, sickness, and death .

སྨོན་ལམ་ནི།
Wishing Prayers

དེ་བཞིན་གཤེགས་པ་ཁྱེད་སྐུ་ཅི་འདྲ་དང་། འཁོར་དང་སྐུ་ཚེའི་
Déshin shékpa kyé ku chi dra tang / khor tang ku tsé'i
ཚད་དང་ཞིང་ཁམས་དང་། ཁྱེད་ཀྱི་མཚན་མཆོག་བཟང་པོ་ཅི་འདྲ་བ།
tsé tang shing kham tang / kyé kyi tsen chok zangpo chi dra wa /
དེ་འདྲ་ཁོ་ན་བདག་སོགས་འགྱུར་བར་ཤོག
dédra khona dasok gyur war sho //

With your excellent manifestation, entourage,
life span, pure realms, and supreme marks,
O Tathagatha, Lord Buddha,
may we come to be like you and you alone.

ཁྱོད་ལ་བསྟོད་ཅིང་གསོལ་བ་བཏབ་པའི་མཐུས། བདག་སོགས་གང་དུ་གནས་པའི་
Kyöla töshing sölwa tab pa'i tü / dasok gangdu népé
ས་ཕྱོགས་སུ། ནད་གདོན་དབུལ་འཕོང་ཐབས་རྩོད་ཞི་བ་དང་།
sa chok su / nédön ülpong tab tsö shiwa tang /
ཆོས་དང་བཀྲ་ཤིས་འཕེལ་བར་མཛད་དུ་གསོལ།
chö tang tashi pelwar dzé du söl //

By the power of having honored and prayed to you,
please pacify illness, malevolence, poverty, and conflicts,
and cause the Dharma and all that is favorable to increase,
wherever we may happen to be.

།འགྲོ་བའི་སྡུག་བསྔལ་སྨན་གཅིག་པུ། །བདེ་བ་ཐམས་ཅད་འབྱུང་བའི་གནས།

Drowé du ngal men chik pu / déwa tamché jungwé né /

བསྟན་པ་རྙེད་དང་བཀུར་སྟི་དང་། །བཅས་ཏེ་ཡུན་རིང་གནས་གྱུར་ཅིག།

tenpa nyé tang kurti tang / chété yunring né gyur chik //

The holy teachings are the unique remedy for the suffering of beings,
and the source of every form of happiness.
May they be supported, may they be held in the highest regard,
and may they endure for a very long time.

བཀྲ་ཤིས།
Wish for Good Fortune

སྟོན་པ་འཇིག་རྟེན་ཁམས་སུ་བྱོན་པ་དང་།
Tönpa jikten kham su jönpa tang /
བསྟན་པ་ཉི་འོད་བཞིན་དུ་གསལ་བ་དང་།
tenpa nyi ö shindu salwa tang /
བསྟན་འཛིན་བུ་སློབ་དར་ཞིང་རྒྱས་པ་ཡིས།
tenzin bu lob darshing gyé pa yi /
བསྟན་པ་ཡུན་རིང་གནས་པའི་བཀྲ་ཤིས་ཤོག།
tenpa yunring népé tashi sho //

With the Buddhas, the Teachers, appearing in the universe,
with the Dharma, the teachings, shining forth like sun and moon,
with disciples, holders of the teachings, increasing and flourishing,
may the great blessing of the Buddhadharma be with us evermore!

Translator's postscript

There are bound to be translation mistakes in this practice text.
I ask the Enlightened Ones to grant me their patience and clemency,
and request their blessing for more wisdom in future endeavors.

Appendix I

Images of the 35 Buddhas

01

ཤཱཀྱ་ཐུབ་པ།

Shakya Tubpa

(Buddha Shakyamuni)

Sanskrit: Bhagavan Shakyamuni Tatagathayarhat Samyak Sambuddha

Translation: Sage of the Shakyas

Color: Golden

Position: Seated in the center

World: *Planet Earth*

02

རྡོ་རྗེའི་སྙིང་པོས་རབ་ཏུ་འཇོམས་པ།

Dorjé nyingpö rabtu jompa

Sanskrit: Vajrasara Pramarda

Translation: He Who Conquers All Through Vajra-Essence

Color: Blue

Position: Seated directly above Buddha Shakyamuni

World: Namkhaï Nyingpo'i Shing
Essence of Space World

03

རིན་ཆེན་འོད་འཕྲོ།

Rinchen ötro

Sanskrit: Ratnarci

Translation: Jewel of Radiant Light

Color: White

Position: Seated in the East, in front of Buddha Shakyamuni

World: Rinchen Yöpé Shing

World Endowed with Jewels

04

ཀླུ་དབང་གི་རྒྱལ་པོ།

Luwangi gyalpo

Sanskrit: Nageshvara Raja

Translation: King of the Powerful Nagas

Color: Blue

Position: Seated in the South-East

World: Luyi Kyabpé Shing

World Filled with Nagas

05

དཔའ་བོའི་སྡེ།

Pawo'i dé

Sanskrit: Virasena
Translation: He of the Heroes
Color: Yellow
Position: Seated in the South
World: Pawo Tang Denpé Shing
World of Heroes

06

དཔལ་དགྱེས།

Palgyé

Sanskrit: Virananda
Translation: Joyful Glory
Color: Orange
Position: Seated in the South-West
World: Gawa Tang Denpé Shing
World of Happiness

07

རིན་ཆེན་མེ།

Rinchen mé

Sanskrit: Ratnagni
Translation: Jewel of Fire
Color: Red
Position: Seated in the West
World: Nangwa Dang Denpe Shing
World of Light

08

རིན་ཆེན་ཟླ་འོད།

Rinchen da ö

Sanskrit: Ratnachandraprabha
Translation: Jewel of Moonlight
Color: White
Position: Seated in the North-West
World: Ö Zangpo'i Shing
World of Excellent Light

09

མཐོང་བ་དོན་ཡོད།

Tongwa dönyö

Sanskrit: Amoghadarsha
Translation: Meaningful to Behold
Color: Green
Position: Seated in the North
World: Nga Dra'i Shing
Sound of Drums World

10

རིན་ཆེན་ཟླ་བ།

Rinchen dawa

Sanskrit: Ratnachandra
Translation: Jewel Moon
Color: Light Green
Position: Seated in the North-East
World: Öser Chen Gyi Shing
World of Light Rays

11

དྲི་མ་མེད་པ།
Drima mépa

Sanskrit: Nirmala
Translation: Immaculate One
Color: Ash Grey
Position: Seated directly below Buddha Shakyamuni
World: Talwé Kyab Pé Shing
World Pervaded by Ashes

12

དཔལ་བྱིན།
Paljin

Sanskrit: Shuradatta
Translation: Gift of Glory
Color: White
Position: Seated two levels above Buddha Shakyamuni
World: Pal Tang Denpé Shing
Glorious World

13

ཚངས་པ།

Tsangpa

Sanskrit: Brahma
Translation: The Pure One
Color: Orange
Position: Seated in the East
World: Dribpa Tang Dralwé Shing
World Free of Obscurations

14

ཚངས་པས་བྱིན།

Tsangpé jin

Sanskrit: Brahmadatta
Translation: Gift of the Pure One
Color: Yellow
Position: Seated in the South-East
World: Nya Ngen Mépé Shing
World Without Torment

15

ཆུ་ལྷ།
Chu lha

Sanskrit: Varuna
Translation: God of the Water
Color: Blue
Position: Seated in the South
World: Drima Mépé Shing
World Without Defilements

16

ཆུ་ལྷའི་ལྷ།
Chu lha'i lha

Sanskrit: Varunadeva
Translation: God of Gods of the Water
Color: White
Position: Seated in the South-West
World: Salwé Shing
World of Clarity

17

དཔལ་བཟང་།

Palzang

Sanskrit: Bhadrashri

Translation: Excellent Glory

Color: Red

Position: Seated in the West

World: Déwachen Gyi Shing

Dewachen: The Blissful World

18

ཙན་དན་དཔལ།

Tsenden pal

Sanskrit: Chandanashri

Translation: Glorious Sandalwood

Color: Orange

Position: Seated in the North-West

World: Dri Zangpö Kyabpé Shing

World Filled with Fine Fragrance

19

གཟི་བརྗིད་མཐའ་ཡས།

Ziji tayé

Sanskrit: Anantaujas

Translation: Infinite Splendor

Color: Red

Position: Seated in the North

World: Ziji Tang Denpé Shing

World of Splendor

20

འོད་དཔལ།

Öpal

Sanskrit: Prabhasashri

Translation: Glorious Light

Color: White

Position: Seated in the North-East

World: Dönyö Tang Denpé Shing

Meaningful World

21

མྱ་ངན་མེད་པའི་དཔལ།

Nya ngen mépé pal

Sanskrit: Ashokashri
Translation: Glory Free from Torment
Color: Light Blue
Position: Seated below Buddha Sakyamuni
World: Dribpa Tang Dralwé Shing
World Free of Obscurations

22

སྲེད་མེད་ཀྱི་བུ།

Sémékyi bu

Sanskrit: Naryana
Translation: Son of No Desire
Color: Blue
Position: Seated above Buddha Sakyamuni
World: Sépa Tang Dralwé Shing
World without Desire

23

མེ་ཏོག་དཔལ།

Métok pal

Sanskrit: Kusumashri

Translation: Glorious Flower

Color: Yellow

Position: Seated in the East

World: Metog Chérgyépa Shéjawé Shing

World Called "Of Fully Blooming Flowers"

24

དེ་བཞིན་གཤེགས་པ་ཚངས་པའི་འོད་ཟེར་རྣམ་པར་རོལ་པ་མངོན་པར་མཁྱེན་པ།

Déshin shékpa tsangpé öser nampar rölpa ngönpar kyenpa

Sanskrit: Brahmajyotivikriditabhigna Tathagata

Translation: Buddha Light of the Pure One, Manifold Display of Manifest Clairvoyance

Color: White

Position: Seated in the South-East

World: Tsangpé Kyabpé Shing

World Pervaded by Purity

25

དེ་བཞིན་གཤེགས་པ་པདྨའི་འོད་ཟེར་
རྣམ་པར་རོལ་པ་མངོན་པར་མཁྱེན་པ།

Déshin shékpa pémé öser nampar rölpa ngönpar kyenpa

Sanskrit: Padmajyotivikriditabhigna Tathagata

Translation: Buddha Light of the Lotus, Manifold Display of Manifest Clairvoyance

Color: Red

Position: Seated in the South

World: Péma Tang Denpé Shing
World with Lotuses

26

ནོར་དཔལ།

Norpal

Sanskrit: Dhanashri

Translation: Wealth of Glory

Color: Red with white sheen

Position: Seated in the South-West

World: Norbu Yöpé Shing
World with Jewels

27

དྲན་པའི་དཔལ།

Drenpé pal

Sanskrit: Smritishri

Translation: Glory of Vigilance

Color: Yellow

Position: Seated in the West

World: Salwa Tang Denpé Shing
World of Clarity

28

མཚན་དཔལ་ཤིན་ཏུ་ཡོངས་གྲགས།

Tsenpal shintu yongdrak

Sanskrit: Suparikirtitanamadheyashri

Translation: Sign of Glory that Proclaims Throughout

Color: Green

Position: Seated in the North-West

World: Tsenma Mépé Shing
World Without Characteristics

29

དབང་པོའི་ཏོག་གི་རྒྱལ་མཚན་གྱི་རྒྱལ་པོ།

Wangpo'i toki gyaltsen gyi gyalpo

Sanskrit: Indraketudvajaraja

Translation: King of the Royal Banner of the Pinnacle of Power

Color: Yellow

Position: Seated in the North

World: Wangpo Salwé Shing

World of Clear Senses

30

ཤིན་ཏུ་རྣམ་པར་གནོན་པའི་དཔལ།

Shintu nampar nönpé pal

Sanskrit: Suvikrantashri

Translation: Glory Who Utterly Overcomes

Color: White

Position: Seated in the North-East

World: Rölpa Tang Denpé Shing

World of Creative Manifestation

31

གཡུལ་ལས་ཤིན་ཏུ་རྣམ་པར་རྒྱལ་བ།

Yüllé shintu nampar gyalwa

Sanskrit: Suvijitasamgrama

Translation: Absolute Victor of Battles

Color: Black

Position: Seated below Buddha Shakyamuni

World: Nyönmongpa Mépé Shing

World Free of Emotional Obscurations

32

རྣམ་པར་གནོན་པས་གཤེགས་པའི་དཔལ།

Nampar nönpé shékpé pal

Sanskrit: Vikrantagamishri

Translation: Buddha Who Overcomes Completely

Color: White

Position: Seated in the East

World: Pal Tang Denpé Shing

Glorious World

33

ཀུན་ནས་སྣང་བ་བཀོད་པའི་དཔལ།

Künné nangwa köpé pal

Sanskrit: Samantavabhasavyuhashri

Translation: Glorious Array of All that Appears

Color: Yellow

Position: Seated in the South

World: Nangwa Köpé Shing

Array of Manifestation World

34

རིན་ཆེན་པདྨ་རྣམ་པར་གནོན་པ།

Rinchen péma nampar nönpa

Sanskrit: Ratnapadmavikrami

Translation: Precious Lotus that Utterly Overcomes

Color: Red

Position: Seated in the West

World: Pal Tang Denpé Shing

Glorious World

35

རིན་པོ་ཆེ་དང་པདྨའི་གདན་ལ་
རབ་ཏུ་བཞུགས་པ་རི་དབང་གི་རྒྱལ་པོ།

Rinpoché tang pémé den la
rabtu shukpa riwangi gyalpo

Sanskrit: Ratnapadmasupratishtitas-hailendraraja Tathagatayar-hate Samyaksambuddha

Translation: King of the Powerful Mountain Who Abides Perfectly on a seat of Jewel Lotus

Color: Sky Blue

Position: Seated in the North

World: Rinpoché'i Shing
World of Jewels

Appendix II

Recitation Options for Homage to 35 Buddhas

Concerning the recitation of the names of the 35 Buddhas, practitioners are encouraged to recite in Tibetan or Sanskrit, as pronunciation of the names carries special blessing. Reciting in English in order to have a clearer vision of the meaning of the names is also fine from time to time, if so desired. In Tibetan, the text may be recited as presented or titles may be added to each Buddha's name. In any case, the names of the first and last Buddha must be recited in full.

It may be easier to concentrate on memorizing the root names first and adding the lengthy titles later if so desired. Je Tsongkhapa suggests that reciting the full title before each name gives the greatest merit.

In Tibetan, the different possibilities are as follows:

A. Recitation as written

1) བཅོམ་ལྡན་འདས་དེ་བཞིན་གཤེགས་པ་དགྲ་བཅོམ་པ་ཡང་དག་པར་རྫོགས་པའི་སངས་རྒྱས་ཤཱཀྱ་ཐུབ་པ་ལ་ཕྱག་འཚལ་ལོ།

2) རྡོ་རྗེའི་སྙིང་པོས་རབ་ཏུ་འཇོམས་པ་ལ་ཕྱག་འཚལ་ལོ།

3) རིན་ཆེན་འོད་འཕྲོ་ལ་ཕྱག་འཚལ་ལོ།

4) ཀླུ་དབང་གི་རྒྱལ་པོ་ལ་ཕྱག་འཚལ་ལོ།

1) Chomdendé déshin shékpa drachompa yangdakpar dzokpé sangyé shakya tubpa la chak tsallo /

2) Dorjé nyingpö rabtu jompa la chak tsallo /

3) Rinchen ötro la chak tsallo /

4) Luwangi gyalpo la chak tsallo /

etc.

B. More extensive recitation

1) བཅོམ་ལྡན་འདས་དེ་བཞིན་གཤེགས་པ་དགྲ་བཅོམ་པ་ཡང་དག་པར་རྫོགས་པའི་སངས་རྒྱས་ཤཱཀྱ་ཐུབ་པ་ལ་ཕྱག་འཚལ་ལོ།

2) རྫོགས་པའི་སངས་རྒྱས་རྡོ་རྗེའི་སྙིང་པོས་རབ་ཏུ་འཇོམས་པ་ལ་ཕྱག་འཚལ་ལོ།

3) རྫོགས་པའི་སངས་རྒྱས་རིན་ཆེན་འོད་འཕྲོ་ལ་ཕྱག་འཚལ་ལོ།

4) རྫོགས་པའི་སངས་རྒྱས་ཀླུ་དབང་གི་རྒྱལ་པོ་ལ་ཕྱག་འཚལ་ལོ།

1) Chomdendé déshin shékpa drachompa yangdakpar dzokpé sangyé shakya tubpa la chak tsallo /

2) Dzokpé sangyé dorjé nyingpö rabtu jompa la chak tsallo /

3) Dzokpé sangyé rinchen ötro la chak tsallo /

4) Dzokpé sangyé luwangi gyalpo la chak tsallo /

etc.

C. Most extensive recitation

1) བཅོམ་ལྡན་འདས་དེ་བཞིན་གཤེགས་པ་དགྲ་བཅོམ་པ་ཡང་དག་པར་རྫོགས་པའི་སངས་རྒྱས་ཤཱཀྱ་ཐུབ་པ་ལ་ཕྱག་འཚལ་ལོ།

2) བཅོམ་ལྡན་འདས་དེ་བཞིན་གཤེགས་པ་དགྲ་བཅོམ་པ་ཡང་དག་པར་རྫོགས་པའི་སངས་རྒྱས་རྡོ་རྗེའི་སྙིང་པོས་རབ་ཏུ་འཇོམས་པ་ལ་ཕྱག་འཚལ་ལོ།

3) བཅོམ་ལྡན་འདས་དེ་བཞིན་གཤེགས་པ་དགྲ་བཅོམ་པ་ཡང་དག་པར་རྫོགས་པའི་སངས་རྒྱས་རིན་ཆེན་འོད་འཕྲོ་ལ་ཕྱག་འཚལ་ལོ།

4) བཅོམ་ལྡན་འདས་དེ་བཞིན་གཤེགས་པ་དགྲ་བཅོམ་པ་ཡང་དག་པར་རྫོགས་པའི་སངས་རྒྱས་ཀླུ་དབང་གི་རྒྱལ་པོ་ལ་ཕྱག་འཚལ་ལོ།

1) *Chomdendé déshin shékpa drachompa yangdakpar dzokpé sangyé shakya tubpa la chak tsallo /*

2) *Chomdendé déshin shékpa drachompa yangdakpar dzokpé sangyé dorjé nyingpö rabtu jompa la chak tsallo /*

3) *Chomdendé déshin shékpa drachompa yangdakpar dzokpé sangyé rinchen ötro la chak tsallo /*

4) *Chomdendé déshin shékpa drachompa yangdakpar dzokpé sangyé luwangi gyalpo la chak tsallo /*

etc.

Appendix III

Resources for Mandala Offering Practice

The Universe

1. Iron Mountains
2. Ocean
3. Seven Mountain Ranges
4. Seven Lakes
5. Mount Meru
6. Purvavideha with Deha and Videha
7. Jambudvipa with Camara and Aparacamara
8. Aparagodaniya with Shatha and Uttaramantrina
9. Uttarakuru with Kurava and Kaurava
10. God Realms
11. Sun
12. Moon

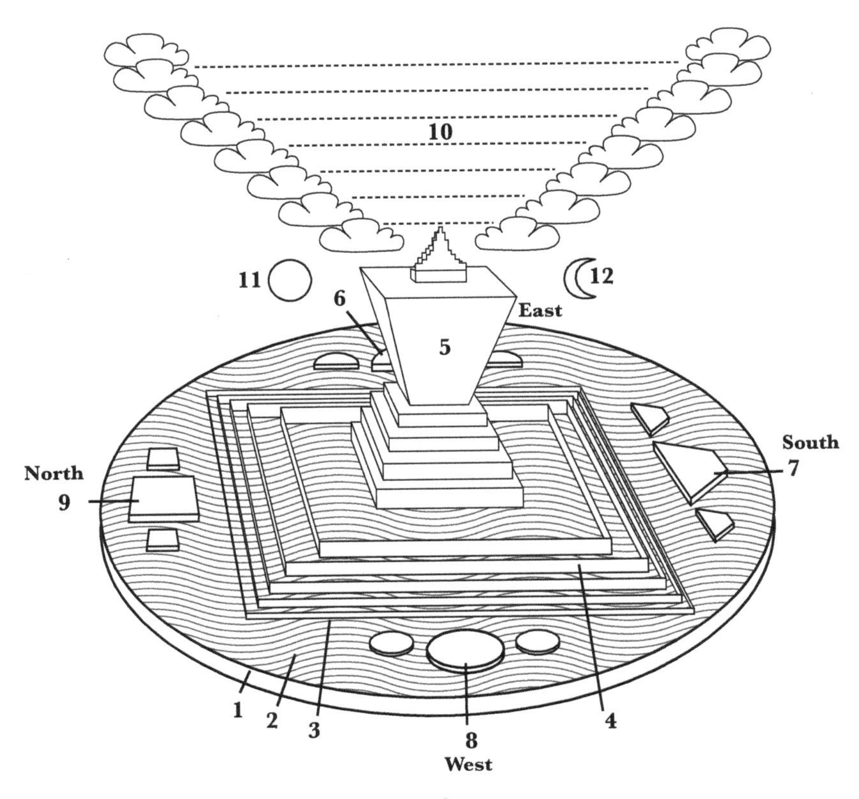

37-Point Mandala Offering

1. Mount Meru
2. Purvavideha
3. Jambudvipa
4. Aparagodaniya
5. Uttarakuru
6. Deha
7. Videha
8. Camara
9. Aparacamara
10. Shatha
11. Uttaramantrina
12. Kurava
13. Kaurava
14. Jewel mountain
15. Wish fulfilling tree
16. Bountiful cow
17. Effortless harvest
18. Precious wheel
19. Precious gem
20. Precious queen
21. Precious minister
22. Precious elephant
23. Fine & precious horse
24. Precious general
25. Great treasure vase
26. Goddess of grace
27. Goddess of garlands
28. Goddess of song
29. Goddess of dance
30. Goddess of flowers
31. Goddes of incense
32. Goddess of light
33. Goddess of perfume
34. Sun
35. Moon
36. Precious parasol
37. Royal banner

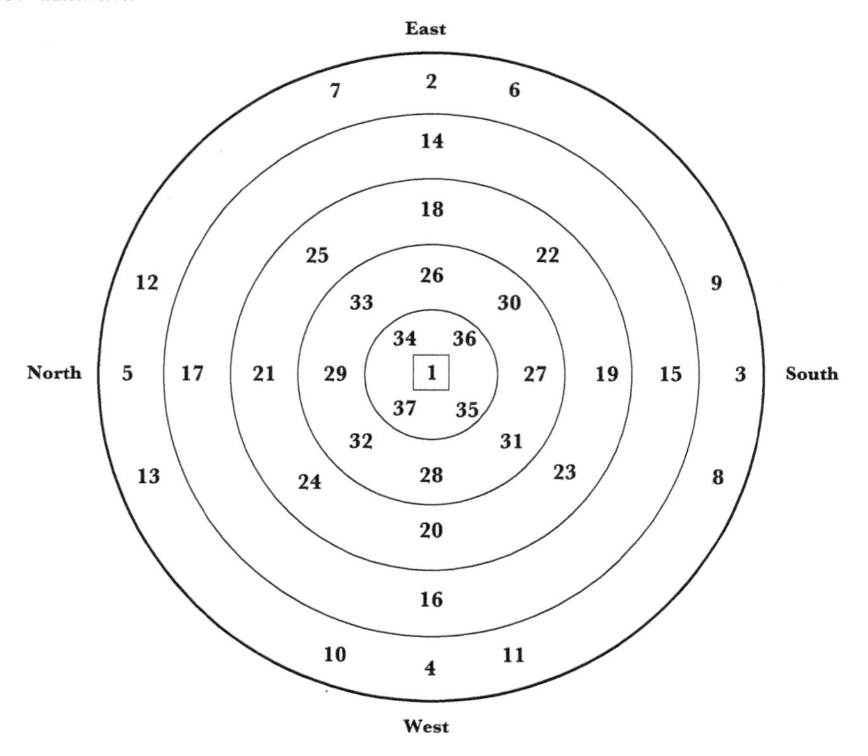

7-Point Mandala Offering

1. Mount Meru
2. Purvavideha
3. Jambudvipa
4. Aparagodaniya
5. Uttarakuru
6. Sun
7. Moon

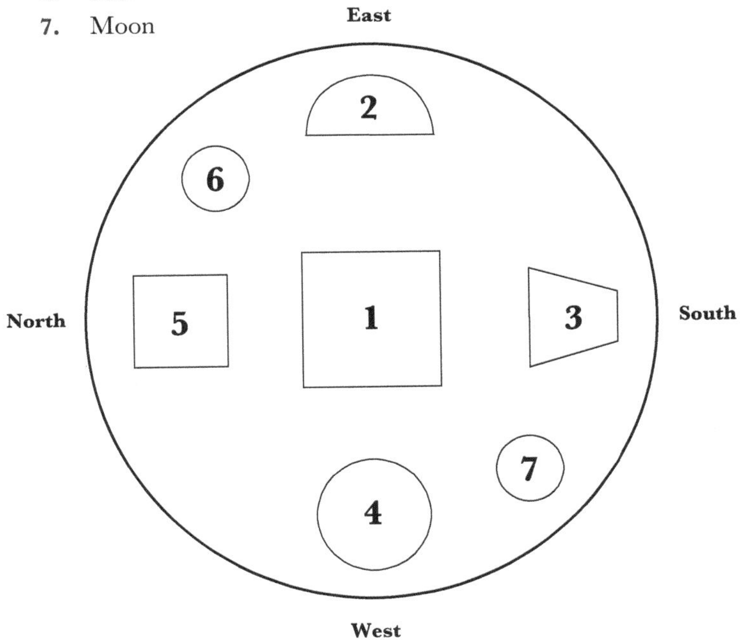

Sashi pöchü juk shing métok tram / Rirab ling shi nyidé gyen pa di /
Sangyé shing du mikté pülwa yi / Drokün namdak shing la chöpar sho //

This ground, sprinkled with perfumed water,
strewn with flowers, adorned with Mount Meru,
the four continents, the sun, and the moon:
I imagine it as a Buddha field and offer it
so that all beings may experience the pure realms.

Printed in the USA
CPSIA information can be obtained
at www.ICGtesting.com
LVHW061047280124
769766LV00006B/6